Woman of

Independence

The Life of
ABIGAIL ADAMS

Other books by Susan Provost Beller:

Roots for Kids: A Genealogy Guide for Young People

Cadets at War: The True Story of Teenage Heroism at the Battle of New Market

Woman of Independence

The Life of ABIGAIL ADAMS

Susan Provost Beller

AN AUTHORS GUILD BACKINPRINT.COM EDITION

AN AUTHORS GUILD BACKINPRINT.COM EDITION

Published by iUniverse.com, Inc.

For information address:
iUniverse.com, Inc.
620 North 48th Street, Suite 201
Lincoln, NE 68504-3467
www.iuniverse.com

Originally published by Shoe Tree Press

ISBN: 0-595-00789-9

Printed in the United States of America

This book is dedicated to my son
SEAN TRISTAN BELLER
Who has been a fan of
Abigail and John
ever since he played John in his
fourth grade play.

ACKNOWLEDGMENTS

It is appropriate that this book begins with a thank you to Judith McAlister Curtis, Curator of the Adams National Historical Site. Her love for and knowledge of Abigail Adams shone through on a very special tour of the Adams' houses that she gave me one Saturday morning. She also fulfilled a lifelong dream of mine when she said, "Would you like me to remove the gate so you can go into the room?" I have always wanted to go beyond the gates and up the stairs to the closed-off parts of historic houses — and this time I did! Judy also was the source of many of the photos included in this book.

My thanks also to Virginia Smith, the reference librarian at the Massachusetts Historical Society. I appreciate her advice and her assistance in putting me in contact with other people I needed to see at the Society to arrange for the use of letters and photographs.

My husband served as photographer for many of the pictures in this book; when I think of this book I will always remember him maneuvering under the roof rafters to get a good picture of the attic area where the three Adams' boys slept as children. He is also the detail reader for the manuscript—the one who tightens up the sloppy writing in my drafts. My colleague at the Bristol Elementary School Library, Dee Corkins, also served as a reader and her comments made me realize that I really did have to bring John Adams more into Abigail's story. My three children, Mike, Jennie, and Sean, also provided their comments on the book at its draft stage. ("You know, it might help to put verbs in your sentences.") Sean was also my companion on a research trip to Boston in which we finally figured out how to get back on Storrow Drive heading north.

PREFACE

rowing up in New England, I learned a lot in school about the American Revolution and about the role of famous Massachusetts men, like John Adams, in helping to found our new country. But all the time I was learning about these men, I wondered what the women were doing. Especially in learning about John Adams, who spent so much of his time helping to build a new nation, I wondered about his wife, Abigail, and why she wasn't getting her share of the glory. Over the years, many books have been published about Abigail Adams, as people have recognized what an extraordinary woman she was. But I've always wanted to tell her story for young adults, using her own letters to speak for her.

To understand Abigail's story, the reader does have to know just what John was doing during these years. The time line included in the book will help you to know where John is and what Abigail is doing during the long years of their marriage. John became one of the most important people in the early history of our new nation. He was appointed to the Continental Congress by the colonial legislature as a delegate from the Massachusetts colony in June 1774. From the time he

ABIGAIL AND JOHN ADAMS TIMELINE

Year	Abigail	Together	John
1764		Married Oct. 25	
1768		Moved to Boston	
1771		Moved to Braintree	
1772		Moved to Boston	
1774	Braintree		Pennsyvania
	"		(Cont. Congress)
1775	"	*	
1776	"	*	
1777	"	*	
1778	"		France (Alliance)
1779	"	*	
1780	"		Netherlands
1781	"	*	
1782	"		Neth./France
1783	"		France
			(Peace Treaty)
1784	To Europe-June	France	
1785		France/Grt. Brit.	
1786		Grt. Brit.	
1787		Grt. Brit.	
1788		Grt. Brit./Mass.	
1789		Philadelphia **	
1790		Philadelphia	
1791	Quincy (4 mos)	Philadelphia	Philadelphia
1792	Quincy		Philadelphia
1793	"		"
1794	"		"
1795	"		"
1796	"		"
1797	Quincy (8 mos)	Philadelphia	"
1798	Quincy (4 mos)	Phil. (4 mos)	Phil. (4 mos)
1799	Quincy (8 mos)	Philadelphia	Phil. (6 mos)
1800		Philadelphia/Quincy/	
		Washington, D.C.	
1801-1818		Quincy	

* Indicates some vacation time together.

** Beginning in 1789, both Abigail and John always spent summers together in Quincy.

left in August, he would not be a regular resident of Massachusetts until he returned as a retired President in 1801. He would serve as a delegate to both Continental Congresses. It was he who would nominate George Washington as Commander of the Continental Army during the American Revolution. He was appointed, along with Thomas Jefferson, to write the Declaration of Independence, but he refused, feeling that it would be more successful if it were written by a Southerner. He would return home several times, but always he would leave again to serve his country. In November 1777, he was picked by Congress to go to France to represent the new nation's interests there. He would not return home until 1788. During that time, he would serve as a negotiator for trade treaties in several countries and eventually become the first American Ambassador to Great Britain. Abigail did join him abroad in 1784, but in the years before, she was alone raising their children and caring for their farm. John was elected the first Vice President of the United States in 1788 and then followed George Washington as the second President of the United States in 1796.

The rest of the book belongs to Abigail ...

Portrait of Abigail, painted by Benjamin Blyth two years after she married John. She was twenty-two years old. (Courtesy of the Massachusetts Historical Society.)

The companion portrait to the one of Abigail, painted by Blyth at the same time. John was thirty-one when this was done. (Courtesy of the Massachusetts Historical Society.)

CONTENTS

Chapter 1

CHILD

ike most people, when Abigail Adams was growing up she had no idea that she would ever become famous. She did not think she was so wonderful that people would know about her 200 years later. She did not think she was so wise that people would want to read the 2000 letters she left behind. She never realized that people would find in her words a most accurate and human picture of the times in which she lived. She would have been shocked to know that people would decide 200 years later that she was one of the greatest voices for women's rights at the time of the American Revolution. If anything, as a child she was frustrated that no one would let her go to school to study. She was embarrassed that everyone would think of her as stupid because she couldn't write and speak well.

Abigail Smith was born in Weymouth, Massachusetts on November 11, 1744 (under the old calendar, that is—her birth date under our current calendar would be November 22). Her father, William Smith, was a well-educated minister at the Congregational Church in Weymouth. He was a man who valued education and was also very tolerant of other people and their ideas. He would not be afraid to educate his daughters even though other people thought education for girls was a terrible idea and would only make them unsuitable wives. Abigail's mother, Elizabeth Quincy, was fourteen years younger than Abigail's father. She came from a family that was already important in the history of the colony of Massachusetts. While growing up, Abigail would have some very important people as relatives. She would be able to see firsthand how people ran the government. She would hear right away about events happening in the Boston area. She would learn from some of the people actually making the decisions.

Abigail was the second child of William and Elizabeth Smith. Her older sister, Mary, was born in 1741. Her only brother, Billy, was born two years after Abigail, in 1746. Her younger sister, Elizabeth, called Betsy, was born in 1750. Abigail was a sickly little girl. This was at a time when many children died young from diseases like consumption, diphtheria, measles, and smallpox. Most parents at the time would know the sorrow of having at least one of their children die. Children who were delicate or sickly were kept at home and not sent to school. People just assumed they would die before they grew up. Abigail remembered later that it seemed she was always sick as a child. She was lucky that none of the illnesses she had at that time were serious enough for her to die. She would live to be seventy-four years old.

Being sick, however, kept her from going to school, even such schooling as girls could have in those days. All her life she would regret her lack of education. But staying home may actually have made her more educated than the girls attending school at the time. Girls attended "dame" schools taught by local women. At the schools girls were taught only enough to read a little and to "cipher" (the simple adding and subtracting they would need to manage a household someday). By staying at home, Abigail had several teachers, and they were very different and much better than those she would have had in dame school.

Abigail's first teacher was her mother. For girls in those days, their mother was always the most important teacher since she would teach them the practical things they would need to know when they ran their own houses. Elizabeth Smith was a perfectionist. She ran her house efficiently and thriftily. She was an excellent minister's wife and always concerned with the needs of her husband's parishioners. She was very capable of handling her own children so that they would never bring shame to their father. She was strict and she believed as others of her time did — that girls should be taught only enough to make them good wives and mothers. Education for women was seen as a waste. Elizabeth Smith would do an excellent job teaching her daughters everything they would need to know to manage their own homes someday. She would also worry that the education her daughters were getting from other people would ruin them as wives and mothers someday. Elizabeth Smith represented well the women of the times. She saw her life as complete in her role as mother and minister's wife. One wonders how she would have felt to have known of the different roles her daughters would play in their own lives.

The Smith girls found their mother to be demanding and overprotective. They conspired together to do things that she would not allow. But as much as they were somewhat annoyed at her restrictions, the girls seemed to have a real affection for their mother. They also appeared to have learned very well all the domestic lessons she taught them. From her mother, Abigail also learned of the need for a strong faith in God. Elizabeth

Smith was a deeply religious person. Her daughters would need her faith to keep them going during some of the experiences they would live through in their own lives.

Abigail's second teacher was her father. William Smith was an exceptionally well-educated man for his time. Abigail became his favorite student. Because she could not attend school, he introduced her to the books he had collected for his library. In colonial times books were very expensive and considered to be luxuries. Most families did not own even one. Those that did own one usually only owned a copy of the Bible. William Smith had collected many books. Unlike the collections of most ministers, his collection included books on a wide variety of different subjects. Abigail's father encouraged her to become a good reader. But, of course, he still did not believe in teaching her things that colonial society felt girls should not know, like Latin. Latin was taught to boys, and it was a required subject for gaining admittance to college. Girls would have no use for something like Latin. Girls only needed to learn simple things.

In fact, Mrs. Smith was afraid her husband was teaching Abigail too many things. People believed that girls who learned too much would not be able to find someone to marry them. Colonial society believed that learning would spoil a girl for marriage because it might make her think she knew as much as her husband. Abigail did not see it that way at all. Abigail had a tremendous hunger for knowledge. All her life she would continue to seek more learning. She would always be open to new experiences and new knowledge.

Abigail had other teachers. Because she could not go to school, she often visited her grandparents' homes for long vacations. Her maternal grandmother, Elizabeth Quincy, who lived only four miles away in Braintree, was her favorite. When she visited the Quincys, she would learn of all the exciting things going on in the big city of Boston. Her grandfather was involved in politics, and sitting at their table, she heard him speak of all the news of the day. He also had lots of visitors, and they were important people. Abigail soaked up everything she heard as the great leaders of Massachusetts debated the issues at her grandfather's house. Grandmother Quincy allowed her to sit on a stool in the corner and listen to the discussions. Grandmother Quincy enjoyed the excitement and she encouraged Abigail to listen and learn also. For Abigail, this exposure to the big world of politics gave her an education that most girls would never have. It also prepared her well for the role she would have as the wife of a political leader. Her encouragement and support of her husband in the political arena would allow him to become one of the leaders of the new nation that would break off from England.

When she visited her other grandparents at their home in Boston, she had a chance to see the world of business. Again, she seemed to soak up all the knowledge that came her way. She delighted in visiting her uncle's warehouse and going down to the wharf to see the big ships being unloaded. Her visits to Boston gave her an interest in the rest of the world. Now she longed to see things for herself. At a time when women seldom left their homes, except to visit relatives, Abigail was getting ready for a future in which she would become a different kind of American woman.

Abigail did end up with one more teacher. Her sister, Mary, was being courted by Richard Cranch. Cranch was skilled in a lot of different areas, but the one that affected Abigail was his love of literature. He introduced Abigail to the literature of the time. He taught her French so she could read in that language.

Cranch had the three Smith sisters reading Shakespeare, Milton, and Pope. These were some of the most important writers of English literature—writers who are still studied in schools today. This was an incredible opportunity for Abigail. Usually, those women who could read only had the chance to read short "moral" stories for women, which stressed that women must live a certain way. To be able to read great literature was something special and more than a little unusual. Again, as with the other parts of her education, Abigail was exposed to ideas and themes that were considered dangerous for women to hear—ideas that might make her think she was equal to the man she would marry. All her life she would give Richard Cranch the credit for her love of literature. All her life she would continue increasing her knowledge of the literature of the day. Her letters would be filled with constant references to the books she was reading.

Richard Cranch would also play another important role in Abigail's life. He would introduce Abigail to the person who would become her "dearest friend," John Adams.

Chapter 2

FRIEND

*J*ohn Adams grew up determined to do something worthwhile with his life. He was a demanding and critical man, not particularly patient with himself or others. He was born in Braintree on October 30, 1735. His parents, John Adams and Susanna Boylston, were demanding of him and he grew up always feeling that he was not achieving enough, no matter what he accomplished. The demands he placed on himself would continue throughout his life. After graduating from Harvard he started out as a schoolmaster, but he was much too ambitious to remain a teacher. He decided to become a lawyer and he proved to be an excellent attorney. He was a forceful speaker with a great deal of knowledge, who could argue for his clients' cases very effectively. He was also an exceptional writer, able to explain his views logically in a way that was persuasive and easy to understand. But he was never happy with himself and always found something to criticize in what he had done. He was most impatient with himself about the time he felt he wasted. He felt he was not a very serious student and that he wasted time when he "gallanted the Girls." The other side of this self-critical personality was his excellent sense of humor. He was

21

This is the front of the Smith parsonage in Weymouth, Massachusetts, where Abigail was born and spent her childhood. (Photo by W. Michael Beller.)

This side view of Abigail's childhood home shows more of its natural setting than the front view. Abigail and John would have spent much time in this yard while they were courting. (Photo by W. Michael Beller.)

known for his ability to imitate people he had seen and to be good enough at it that everyone would be amused.

John courted Hannah Quincy for a while during the summer of 1759. She was the daughter of a fellow lawyer with whom he often met to discuss cases. She was also the cousin of Abigail Smith. John was very much interested in marrying her. Apparently she was very popular and had several men interested in her that same summer, including Richard Cranch. When she decided to marry someone else, John decided he would stop wasting his time courting and spend it improving himself.

But Richard Cranch decided he was interested in courting Mary Smith, the oldest daughter of Reverend Smith of Weymouth. He invited John to come and keep him company as he called on Mary. John reluctantly came along but he was not at all impressed with the Smith girls when he met them in the summer of 1759. He didn't think they compared at all with Hannah Quincy and he described them in his diary as "not fond, not frank, not candid." But he continued to visit the Smith household with Richard Cranch.

John was twenty-six at the time he met Abigail Smith. She was only seventeen. He was very unimpressed with her at first, but as he continued to visit the Smith household with Richard Cranch, he began to like Abigail better. Several years after he met her, John was describing Abigail as "a constant feast ... Prudent, modest, delicate, soft, sensible, obliging, active." His feelings had definitely changed. By the time Mary Smith and Richard Cranch married in November 1762, John's visits to the Smith house were definitely something he looked forward to. Now John was also courting one of the Smith girls.

Abigail seemed to have seen in John right from the beginning the man she wished to marry. But there would be several obstacles along the way. Not only did John develop his liking for her only slowly, but her parents, especially her mother, were also against any marriage between Abigail and John. Abigail was seen as being of a higher social class than John, and her parents thought that she was too good for him. Abigail's grandparents were very important people in the Massachusetts colony; John's were not. Worse still, John himself was a lawyer and lawyers did not have a good reputation in colonial society. In fact, in colonial Massachusetts, lawyers had a terrible reputation as "leeches on society." If he wanted to court Abigail Smith, John would have been better to have stayed a schoolmaster. Her parents thought that she could find someone much more suitable than John. But Abigail and John were persistent and finally her parents agreed. The story of the Smiths' feeling that John was an unacceptable suitor would remain part of family legend in the days after he became one of the most famous Americans and the second President of the United States. Abigail never doubted that she had picked the right man.

Abigail and John would finally marry on October 25, 1764 in Weymouth, Massachusetts. The man whom she called her "dearest friend" in her letters would become her "beloved partner"—it would become one of the most famous partnerships of American history. Many years later, John wrote in his diary of his marriage, describing it as "a connection which has been the source of all my felicity [happiness]."

Chapter 3

WIFE

*O*ver the years, the thing Abigail Adams is probably most remembered for is her unique marriage to John Adams. In a time when the wives of even great men were hardly ever heard from, John and Abigail had a special partnership. Abigail's role in the partnership would be to stay at home as teacher and farmer while John was away. But the partnership was also a political one. From the very beginning, John saw Abigail as a trusted advisor on political matters, as a sounding board for his views, and as a most accurate observer of the political events of the day. They shared an equal passion for the changes happening in their homeland. That shared passion helped them to develop an equality in their marriage that was almost unheard of in their time.

Abigail and John seemed to settle into their life as a couple with incredible ease. They moved into the house in Braintree at the foot of Penn's Hill, which John had inherited when his father died. Their small home was right across the lawn from John's mother's home, and both houses are still standing today. Across the road was a neighbor's home. The three houses were clustered together by the main road to Boston for

This old painting shows the two houses known as the Adams Birthplaces. John Adams was born and grew up in the house on the right. The house on the left was the one he and Abigail moved into when they married. It would be the birthplace of John Quincy Adams. Notice how close to the road the houses are. The road is the main one into Boston. (Courtesy of the U.S. Dept. of the Interior, National Park Service, Adams National Historic Site, Quincy, Massachusetts.)

The parlor of the Braintree house. Notice the painting on the wall of the Adams Birthplaces. (Photo by W. Michael Beller.)

companionship, with their farms behind them. The house was a simple one with two rooms on the first floor, a kitchen and a parlor, and two bedrooms upstairs. John added a shed off the back, which gave them two more rooms on the first floor, including a "modern" kitchen with the oven on the side of the fireplace instead of to the back of the hearth. This was the latest innovation and reduced the danger of a woman's skirts catching fire when she reached into the oven. John turned the old kitchen into an office and began practicing law from his home while at the same time farming his forty acres of land. Upstairs, the rear shed gave them an unfinished attic area off the back of one of the bedrooms, which they would use as a bedroom for their sons.

John loved farming and Abigail began to learn as much as possible about farm management so that she could help John. She found out that farming relaxed John. He spent many happy hours taking care of his orchards or plowing his fields. Abigail took to farm life and proved a good student of all that John taught her about managing a farm. That interest would prove extremely important in the later years when John left home to attend the Continental Congress and then to serve as a representative of the new American government in Europe. Abigail's knowledge of farming that she learned from John in the quiet early years of her marriage would prepare her well for her new job as a "farmeress." John was very impressed with how quickly she learned, and many, many years later he would acknowledge that she had become a better farmer than he ever was.

Their long quiet time farming together during the first years of their marriage also gave them time to develop their political partnership. John delighted in sharing with Abigail all the political news that he heard

John's and Abigail's bedroom in their first home in Braintree (now Quincy). (Photo by W. Michael Beller.)

The only other bedroom on the second floor of the Braintree house. Notice the small doorway leading to the attic space where the Adams boys would sleep. (Photo by W. Michael Beller.)

and lecturing her on the implications of what was happening. He found in Abigail not only an intense interest in what he told her but a keen mind that could match his in their discussions about the news he brought her. Both of them shared a love of reading newspapers and discussing the articles in them. In those days, the newspapers were much more political and were really more of a place to read about people's opinions on political issues — sort of like article-length letters to the editor that other readers would respond to with their own views. John often sent long articles to the papers, and both John and Abigail enjoyed discussing the responses that would appear in later issues. Abigail became John's sounding board as he prepared to write about the issues of the day. Their discussions refined his thinking and helped him to express himself more easily when he wrote.

As John began to become increasingly involved in the political discussion of the times, Abigail began to show her abilities as a gracious hostess. She put to good use her memories of sitting at her Grandmother Quincy's table while listening to her grandfather talk about politics with his important visitors. Now she would have her chance to provide a place for John to entertain influential people of their time.

John's law practice continued to grow and kept him away from home a good deal of the time. Three years into her marriage, Abigail found herself settling into the pattern that would be hers for most of her married life. With John gone, she would work the farm, take care of the children (two of them at this point), visit her relatives, and write letters. She would spend most of her married life waiting for John to come home. In all her later years she would look back on these first few quiet years of their marriage as a very special time in her life.

The area where John Quincy and his younger brothers had to sleep, since the house had only two bedrooms—one for his parents and one for his older sister Nabby. (Photo by W. Michael Beller.)

John had a new, improved kitchen added to the house with a separate oven to the right of the fireplace. Many colonial women died when the oven was inside the back of the fireplace, since their long dresses could catch on fire. John wanted to make sure Abigail had the safer fireplace. (Courtesy of the U.S. Dept. of the Interior, National Park Service, Adams National Historic Site, Quincy, Massachusetts.)

The partnership formed during these early years would be the one that would carry them both through all of their lonely years apart from each other. They would spend over half of their married life away from each other. But even when apart, their strong partnership would hold them together. And never would their times together be as simple and quiet as these first few years together in Braintree.

The Braintree home of John and Abigail Adams as it looks today. (Courtesy of the U.S. Dept. of the Interior, National Park Service, Adams National Historic Site, Quincy, Massachusetts.)

Chapter 4

MOTHER

*M*otherhood came along quickly for Abigail Adams. John and Abigail's first child, a daughter, was born on July 14, 1765. They named her Abigail but she would always be called Nabby. Their first son followed just under two years later, on July 11, 1767. He was named John Quincy Adams after Abigail's favorite grandfather, John Quincy, who died two days after her son was born.

Nabby and John Quincy (called Johnny as a child) spent their earliest life in the house in Braintree, but as John became increasingly involved with his law practice the family moved to Boston in April 1768. As happy as Abigail was to be back in the excitement of Boston, it was also a busy time for her. John and Abigail's third child, a daughter, was born not long after they moved to Boston, on December 28, 1768. They named her Susanna and called her Suky. But Suky was not to be with them for very long. She died on February 4, 1770, not even fourteen months old.

Abigail was already pregnant again when Suky died and her son Charles was born on May 29, 1770. Another son, Thomas Boylston Adams, would follow on September 15, 1772.

For Abigail it must have been an exhausting time. John was increasingly involved in his law career and in the increasing dissatisfaction with King George III that was building in Boston. John and Abigail moved three times within the Boston area as their family grew. Having small children, dealing with pregnancies, and with John busy, it's no wonder Abigail looked back on her earlier time in Braintree as such a special time in her life.

In April 1771, John, near exhaustion, moved his family back to Braintree because he was convinced that living in Boston was too much for both him and his family. But it was not to last. In November 1772, Abigail moved once again into a larger house on Queen Street in Boston. Her four children were now Nabby, seven years old, Johnny, five, Charles, two and a half years, and Tommy, two and one-half months old. This time John promised her they would stay in one place. But less than two years later, John would again move the family back to Braintree before leaving to attend the Continental Congress.

Abigail would experience the sadness of failed motherhood one more time in her life. In July 1777, on Johnny's tenth birthday and with John away at the Continental Congress, Abigail gave birth to a stillborn baby girl. Abigail mourned alone, sharing her pain with John in her letters. People who knew her said the experience deeply affected her. She herself said in her letters to John that it made her feel closer to him and to their four living children. She also reminded him in a letter that in the thirteen years of their marriage, "not more than half that time have we had the happiness of living together." (August 5, 1777.)

Abigail seemed genuinely to enjoy motherhood. She also saw it as a responsibility to be taken seriously. She ordered what books she could find on the subject and became familiar with what was supposed to be the right way to raise children. She even visited Mercy Otis Warren at her home in 1773. Mercy Warren had a reputation for being a model mother. Abigail came away feeling very impressed with how Mercy Warren managed her house. Abigail used what she had seen and read to develop her own philosophy of child-rearing. She would work to raise her children to be useful members of society as adults.

Abigail shared her thoughts about the problems of raising children with her sisters. More than anything else, it seemed to be her correspondence with her mother and sisters that provided the answers she needed for domestic matters. She found her role as a mother to be a fulfilling one. She admitted in a letter to John how she had always been annoyed by people bragging about their children. But she told him that now she found that everything *their* children said and did was exciting to her.

Abigail viewed her role as a mother to be a serious one of preparing her children to be responsible citizens of their nation. We will be seeing in the next chapter how that affected her education of the children. It's important to understand that she saw her role as even more basic than education. She raised her children, especially her sons, to be public figures. Many years later, when John was Vice President, she would write to Tommy: "I consider it one of my chief blessings to have sons worthy of the confidence of their country." (November 8, 1796.) For any mother of the time, this was a sign of a job well done.

John Quincy grew up to be an outstanding success as a diplomat. He would become President of the United States and later serve in Congress. He would be a perfect example of a son raised to serve his country.

Thomas had a difficult time when he was in his

35

twenties in finding the right career. He was also sick with rheumatism much of the time, and Abigail was very worried about him. Eventually he settled down near John and Abigail in Quincy, became a judge, and was their close support in their old age.

But in her other two children she did not always see such success. Her son Charles suffered from alcoholism. He died in 1800 after having misused $6000 given to him by John Quincy to invest. In 1799 when John found out the truth about Charles's problem with alcohol and his misspending of other people's money, he renounced him; Abigail did not. She stood by, grieving at what had become of her son. She visited him just three weeks before he died. Abigail was very supportive of Charles's wife and two daughters. She and John took one daughter, Susanna, into their own household to raise.

Abigail also suffered as she watched Nabby and her difficulties as an adult. Nabby married William Smith. He was always trying to work out some deal that would make him rich. There were times when he would be successful and then Nabby and their children would be secure for a while. But then he would spend what they had in trying to make even more money, and lose it all. Abigail and John grieved as they watched Nabby and her children suffer through his actions. They were often left with nothing to live on while William went away to make his fortune. Abigail always believed that the fault was William's. She helped out whenever and wherever possible, taking her grandsons into her own household for a while and providing a refuge for Nabby when she needed one.

The letters between Abigail and Nabby show that they were close to each other, especially as the years went on. But Abigail's letters were also often nagging ones, especially in the first years. For a long time,

Nabby looked to her Aunt Mary Cranch, who was less critical of her, for support rather than to Abigail. But over the years, Abigail and Nabby became much closer. The slow, painful death of her daughter from cancer in 1813 was a terrible experience for Abigail. Nabby finally died in the Adamses' home in Quincy in the bedroom next to her parents' room, with William arriving to take care of her only at the very last moment.

Abigail was a good but strict and demanding mother to her children. She loved her children very much, but that feeling comes through more in her letters to them as adults than in her letters about them as children. When Thomas was away from her for three years in Europe, she would end a letter to him with warm feelings, but expressed in the stiff words of the time: "Neither time, absence or sickness have lessened the warmth of her affection for her dear children, which will burn with undiminished fervour until the lamp of life is extinguished." (November 8, 1796.)

Chapter 5

TEACHER

*A*bigail Adams, like her mother before her, in time became the teacher of her own children. With John's absence, first for the Continental Congress and later for treaty negotiations and as an ambassador, Abigail would be the most important educational influence in their children's lives.

When John left for the Continental Congress in August of 1774, he and Abigail divided up the duties of their partnership for the short time he thought he would be away. John and Abigail had been married now for just under ten years, and so far they had followed the traditional arrangement of the time with John directing all of Abigail's activities. With his departure, this would change. John would be a statesman and would help in the birth and development of this new nation. Abigail would run the farm and the family. She would assume the task of keeping the money coming in so that they could eat. She was also given the task of educating their children to her and John's standards.

This was somewhat different from Elizabeth Smith's role in educating her children so many years before. But Abigail, as always, was up to the challenge.

Abigail and John both felt that the education of their children was very important. Although John would only be home occasionally over the years, he wrote to Abigail constantly, giving her instructions on how he wanted the children to be educated. Their letters give us a chance to see what things they felt were important for their children to learn.

When he was younger, John had been very disgusted with himself for the time he felt he had wasted in not being a serious student. Now he was determined that his own sons be hard-working and industrious. He wanted them to be ambitious, honest, just, and moral persons. They also had to be physically strong. In addition to all the usual subjects like Latin and Greek that boys studied, he wanted them to learn French, which he had never learned. It was important to him that they be good writers (which he was). He insisted that they begin writing at a young age and that Abigail be very quick in correcting any errors they made in writing.

When John first left, two law clerks lived with the family and carried on part of John's law practice. One of them was a cousin of Abigail's, John Thaxter, and he helped to tutor young John Quincy in the normal school subjects of the day. But Abigail provided the schooling in the less formal subjects such as writing and current events. And her influence would prove strong, especially on the life of John Quincy.

Abigail herself felt very strongly about the need for a really good education for all her children, not just her sons. Perhaps some of this came from her belief that her own education had been so poor. Some probably also came from John's constant nagging in his letters. Whatever the reason, Abigail proved to be an excellent teacher, though also a very strict one. Her sister Elizabeth, whose husband ran a school that all Abigail's sons would attend to prepare for admission to Harvard, felt that Abigail was too stern a mother and teacher. She would write to Abigail about how nervous she made John Quincy feel and how demanding Abigail was. But Abigail would not change her mind. She felt that her children should be pushed and she demanded hard work from them.

Her views on education did not soften in any way as she got older. The importance of discipline and learning is a constant theme in her letters to her sisters, her grown children, and her grandchildren. In November 1809, she would write to her sister Elizabeth, "I consider it as an indispensable requisite, that every American wife should herself know how to order and regulate her family; how to govern her domestics, and train up her children." Abigail was still arguing for exactly what she had practiced in teaching her own children.

It is important to remember that even though she was strict, she was also a very good teacher and that she was able to bestow her own love of learning on her children. By the time John Quincy was three, she was teaching him some of her favorite poems. And she believed in reading with her children. She would have John Quincy or Nabby start reading a chapter in a difficult book and then she would take over, finishing the chapter and talking with them about what they had heard. John Quincy, in the opening chapters of an unfinished biography of his father, recalled his mother's teaching. He spoke of how she taught her children her favorite literary works and then gave an example of a patriotic poem that she taught "the writer of this narrative and his brothers, in the days of Lexington and Bunker's Hill." He then quotes the poem from memory.

Abigail believed strongly in teaching her children about the important things that were happening in the world around them. One of the most famous stories about her teaching her children this way is the story of her taking John Quincy to watch the Revolutionary War Battle of Bunker Hill from Penn's Hill near their home. She is supposed to have told her seven-year-old son that one day school children would be reading about this battle in their history books. But she wanted him to be able to say that he had seen the battle himself. She and John Quincy watched together from the hill. Many years later a monument was put up to mark the spot from which the two of them watched. Attached to the stone monument, called a cairn, is a bronze plaque with these words:

From this spot, with her son
JOHN QUINCY ADAMS
Then a boy of seven by her side
ABIGAIL ADAMS
Watched the smoke of Burning Charlestown
While listening to the Guns of Bunker Hill
Saturday, 17 June 1775

This cairn marks the spot from which Abigail and her seven-year-old son, John Quincy, stood and watched the smoke and listened to the guns during the Battle of Bunker Hill on June 17, 1775. (Photo by W. Michael Beller.)

It is a spot people still visit today. Because Abigail was so interested in the historic events of the time, her children probably became some of the best educated children of the time on these subjects.

Abigail also seemed to remember her own time as a child sitting at her Grandfather Quincy's table and listening to him talk with his important visitors about the major political events of the day. Even with John gone, her home became a stopping place for many important people, who would give her the latest political news and listen to what she could tell them about what was happening in Massachusetts. She always made sure her children, especially John Quincy and Nabby, had the chance to hear these discussions and learn from their guests.

No one could say that her children had the typical education of the day. But then again, they also did not have the typical parents of the day. One person writing about Abigail has said that her children grew up thinking their father was someone who only visited them occasionally in between going out and changing the world. As much as they missed their father, these children had probably the most unusual and capable of teachers in their mother. For someone who always felt she was poorly educated, Abigail proved to more than meet John's demands of her as the teacher of their children.

Chapter 6

FARMERESS

*T*he second part of the duties that fell to Abigail when John left was the role of "farmeress," as Abigail jokingly referred to herself. Being the farmeress of the family would be no easy assignment, especially during the Revolutionary War when prices went higher and higher as many items became scarce.

But Abigail had learned well from John in those quiet early years in Braintree. With her keen mind she had learned all the tricks of good farm management. In fact, she would do more than manage the family farm well during the years when he was gone. She would do the job better than John could have done. In her letter to John on April 11, 1776, she wrote, "I find it necessary to be the directress of our husbandry [farming]. I hope in time to have the reputation of being as good a farmeress, as my partner has of being a good statesman."

At times the process of keeping the farm going and her family clothed seemed impossible. She wrote to John of making soap and sewing new clothes. She complained of merchants who were charging unreasonable rates for goods and of things like sugar, molasses, rum, coffee, and chocolate, which were not available at any price. She worked hard to have a surplus of her own crops. She reported to John on all the successes and failures in the neighborhood, including the story of how some women had dealt with John's cousin, Thomas Boylston, who was hoarding goods. They had "seized him by his neck and tossed him into the cart ... tipped up the cart and discharged him, then opened the warehouse, hoisted out the coffee themselves, put it into the truck, and drove off." (July 31, 1777.)

"I endeavor to live in the most frugal manner possible," Abigail wrote to John on July 16, 1775. When the summer of 1778 brought a drought that ruined her corn and potato crops and her orchard, Abigail vowed to John that she was looking for every possible way to survive as she rented out half of the farm and decided to delay buying a new carriage, which had risen to a very high price. She told John she would not pay the prices being charged for fresh meat. She told him many people were resorting to the barter system to obtain goods, as money meant almost nothing now. John encouraged her from a distance, praising her thrift and her business sense.

When John first left, her letters always referred to her care of "your" farm and "your" property. As the years went by it went to "our" farm and "our" property. Eventually she would write of "my" farm. Abigail was increasingly becoming the partner in charge of their financial security instead of just minding the store until her husband's return. By 1780 John no longer even bothered advising her as to purchases, recognizing her greater skill and knowledge. He interfered only once, when she decided to purchase some land in Vermont. This he tried to stop, but Abigail proceeded to buy it with her own money, which she had inherited from her father. They had come a long way from his detailed letters of advice when he first left home.

Even when Abigail later joined John in Europe, she was the one who oversaw their property through letters to her sister Mary. She sent detailed instructions to her sister, covering every aspect of managing her farms and property right down to telling her to make sure the painter Mary hired to do some painting for her was competent. In London she imposed her sense of thrift on the management of their home and on the way that official guests were entertained. Abigail was shocked by the waste she found there and the number of servants required to maintain a modest home. She managed her own household with the three servants less than the "required" eleven for a household her size. She served her guests plain and simple meals. For Abigail, being thrifty had become a basic part of her nature.

As the wife of the Vice President and later President, she set more modest standards for her entertaining than was usual, noting that she could not entertain at the level of the Washingtons, who could spend at a level well beyond the presidential salary. Finally, when it came time for their retirement from public life, it was Abigail who went ahead and arranged their purchase of a larger home in Quincy. She supervised its renovation and expansion as a surprise for John. John was enthusiastic when he found out, to Abigail's relief!

Everyone in the family knew that Abigail was the better business person of the two. When several of John's business deals fell through, it was Abigail's own investments that saved the day for them. What a long way she had come from the young wife learning farm management from her husband.

Chapter 7

PATRIOT

*I*n a letter John wrote to Abigail's sister Mary, while he was courting Abigail, he teasingly referred to her as "A most loyal subject to young George [the King]." (December 30, 1761.) But by the time the revolution came, Abigail was one of its leaders. Abigail's grandson, Charles Francis Adams, who first published her letters, writes of her that, "There was no one, who witnessed his [John's] studies with greater interest, or who sympathized with him in his conclusion, to which his mind was forcing him, more deeply than Mrs. Adams, and ... as the day of trial came, ... she was found not unprepared."

Abigail and John, as part of their partnership, discussed all the political happenings of the day. For Abigail, who had sat at her grandfather's dining room table listening to the leaders of the Massachusetts colony discuss politics, this was the most natural thing in the world. As she and John discussed the events, both of them began to see a need for a change in the way the colonies of England should deal with each other. We think of John Adams as one of the great patriots of the Revolutionary War time period. But it's important to see that Abigail was just as strong a patriot as John.

She wrote a great letter to her friend Mercy Otis Warren in 1773 (two and a half years before the Declaration of Independence), which is as inspiring as any of the words we learn from the Founding Fathers, as they are called, of our new country. She wrote, "The flame is kindled and like lightning it catches from soul to soul. Great will be the devastation if not timely quenched or allayed by some more lenient measures." (December 5, 1773.) She went on to speak of the fact that an actual war might even be necessary. Long before the Revolutionary War began, Abigail was supporting the needs of what would become a new nation.

For Abigail, the time of war was a difficult one. Abigail freely supported John in his decision to offer his services to his country. She wrote to him on May 7, 1776, telling him that "All domestic pleasures and enjoyments are absorbed in the great and important duty you owe your country." But while John was away at the Continental Congress, it was Abigail who had to deal with the day-to-day realities of living in a country moving toward war and later involved in war. Her letters to John tell of all the local unrest, of the conflict between neighbors who supported the King and those, like Abigail, who were opposed to what he was doing. She told John of providing food and a place to rest for soldiers after an exciting morning when a group of British soldiers tried to attack Weymouth. Among the personal items owned by Abigail that still exist today is her bullet mold. The story is told that she melted down her pewter spoons to make bullets during the Revolutionary War. She lived with the constant fear of attack. As the wife of John Adams, their representative at the Continental Congress, people looked to her for leadership and advice.

With John so far away and with both of them having to send their letters by "safe" carriers so that they

A visitor to the Adams Mansion today can see this bullet mold that Abigail is said to have used to make bullets during the Revolutionary War. She melted down her pewter spoons and could make fifteen bullets from every pound of pewter. (Courtesy of the U.S. Dept. of the Interior, National Park Service, Adams National Historic Site, Quincy, Massachusetts.)

would not fall into the hands of the British, Abigail had very little contact with John. She increasingly had to speak for him since she could not get his answers to questions when people needed them. Abigail was so strong a patriot herself and knew so well John's feelings on issues that she was able to speak for him easily and accurately.

Some of what Abigail had to deal with were physical hardships—shortages of foods and other essential goods. It is amusing to read in one of her long, detailed letters to John describing an attack—a really serious letter—a request at the end for him to get her some sewing needles and pins as they had become scarce in Massachusetts and when they could be found, were outrageously expensive. John counted on Abigail to supply him with details on conditions at home. Her letters became a list of items in short supply, persons killed, conditions in Boston, etc. It is obvious how much information Abigail was receiving from local people. Abigail recognized her own part in providing the needed information, referring to herself as a "sister delegate." She was a good reporter—very factual and not at all hysterical. She told John what she knew and always let him know if she was not sure of the accuracy of the information she was sending. After the Battle of Bunker Hill, she shared what information she had and then wrote: "Ten thousand reports are passing, vague and uncertain as the wind ... I am not able to give you any authentic account of last Saturday." (June 20, 1775.)

Abigail also served as John's hostess, meeting and often entertaining friends of John who would come to Massachusetts, such as George Washington and Benjamin Franklin. As time went on, Abigail, dealing with the deaths resulting from clashes between colonists and British troops and the day-to-day hardships of the time, began to be even further ahead of John in her feelings about the need for independence from the King. She wrote to John on November 12, 1775 saying, "Let us separate; they are unworthy to be our brethren. Let us renounce them: and ... let us beseech the Almighty to blast their counsels and bring to nought all their devices." She urged him on, sending him word of the people's displeasure with how slow and conservative the Continental Congress was in taking action on declaring the colonies independent. She wrote to John on May 7, 1776, "The people are all in a flame ... if a king let his people slip from him, he is no longer a king. And as this is most certainly our case, why not proclaim to the world, in decisive terms, your own importance. Shall we not be despised by foreign powers, for hesitating so long at a word?"

Chapter 8

HISTORIAN

*A*bigail Adams was more than just a Revolutionary War patriot. Reading through her letters over two hundred years later, one gets the sense that she served as a chronicler of the Revolutionary War in Massachusetts. Her letters serve as an historical record that presents an accurate picture of events occurring in her area at that time. Her record is equal to, and in many way surpasses, the other existing accounts. We have already seen some of this in reading part of one of her letters to John about the battle for Charlestown. But there is much more there that makes fascinating reading to anyone interested in the Revolutionary War time period.

Abigail's strength as an historian lies in her descriptions of events and in the details she provides. Her feelings show through strongly, but she always tries to keep her facts correct. In a letter to John, dated July 5, 1775, she wrote: "The present state of the inhabitants of Boston is that of the most abject slaves. Among many instances I could mention, let me relate one. Upon the 17th of June, printed handbills were posted up at the corners of the streets and upon houses, forbidding any inhabitants to go upon their houses, or upon any eminence, on pain of death; the inhabitants dared not to look out of their houses, nor to be heard or seen to ask a question." She continues with a detailed depiction of the lives of citizens of Boston, noting their lack of basic necessities with her statement, "Their living cannot be good, as they have no fresh provisions; their beef, we hear, is all gone, and their wounded men die very fast, so that they have a report that the bullets were poisoned." She and John still owned a house in Boston during the Revolutionary War, so she would want Boston news and would, of course, share it with John in her letters.

But her descriptions go beyond just a summary of details—she captures the actual feelings of that time and place. In May 1775, she wrote John of threats against patriots by the British: "They have taken a list of all those who they suppose were concerned in watching the tea, [this refers to the Boston Tea Party of December 16, 1773, when Boston inhabitants threw over three hundred chests of British tea into the harbor to protest taxes] and every other person whom they call obnoxious, and they and their effects are to suffer destruction." It is not hard to imagine the worry of the people who will be targeted by the British after reading her account as she prays for "the interposition of Heaven in their favor."

On July 16, 1775, she reported to John the news given to her by a goldsmith who had just escaped from Boston: "Their beef is all spent; their malt and cider all gone. All the fresh provisions they can procure, they are obliged to give to the sick and wounded." In October 1775, she wrote to John with information from another man who had managed to escape from Boston. She wrote of what he told her: "No language can paint the distress of the inhabitants; most of them are destitute of wood and provisions of every kind. The bakers say, unless they have a new supply of wood, they cannot bake above one fortnight longer; their biscuit are not above one half the former size ... The inhabitants are desperate, and contriving means of escape." In letter after letter, she detailed the increasing hardships of the people of Boston and the damage caused by the occupying British Army. She even finds out that their home in Boston is being used to house British soldiers. The picture of the situation in Boston as it worsens is vividly described in her letters to John.

In those same letters to John, Abigail provides a military history of the Boston area during the war, from the time when John leaves up to the point when the British sail out of Boston in March 1776 and the Revolutionary War fighting moves south. On September 14, 1774, one month after John left as a delegate to the Continental Congress, she wrote of the beginning of the siege of Boston: "The Governor is making all kinds of warlike preparations, such as mounting cannon upon Beacon Hill, digging intrenchments upon the Neck, placing cannon there, encamping a regiment there, throwing up breast works." She informs John in the same letter that the townspeople of Braintree have also begun their preparations for war. She wrote that "two hundred men ... marched down to the powderhouse, from whence they took the powder, and carried it into the other parish and there secreted it" to protect the town's supply of gunpowder from possible capture by the British or their sympathizers.

By the following spring, the British are on the march and the first shots of the American Revolution are fired. In Braintree, there is as yet no action. But Abigail's letters to John continue the account, even when there is no real news to report: "Things remain much the same here ... There has been no descent upon the seacoast." (May 4, 1775.)

In May 1775, the inhabitants of Braintree have their

first real scare from the British, and Abigail shares the excitement and worry of the event in a letter to John on May 24, 1775. The British came by boats to collect hay on an island just offshore from Braintree. Abigail wrote of the drums and the alarms as the townspeople discovered that "Three sloops and one cutter had come out and dropped anchor just below Great Hill." She also captures the confusion and the inaccurate rumors that were flying about, "that three hundred had landed, and were upon their march up into town." Two thousand patriots gathered to defend the town, according to Abigail's report, only to find that they could not get at the British on the island since they lacked boats. The townspeople did have a military victory of sorts, firing at the soldiers and preventing them from taking much hay at all. Eventually a few small boats were filled with men and, in Abigail's words, "Our people landed upon the island, and in an instant set fire to the hay, which, with the barn, was soon consumed." The result was eighty tons of hay destroyed, with the British taking only about three tons. Historian Abigail's account is specific and captures well the minor skirmish and the reactions of the townspeople.

By June, as the tension has increased, Abigail's letters advise John of the state of alertness within the area, "We now expect our seacoast ravaged; perhaps the very next letter I write will inform you that I am driven away from our yet quiet cottage." (June 15, 1775.) Three days later, Abigail has real news as she writes to John of the fighting in Boston: "The battle began upon our intrenchments upon Bunker's Hill, Saturday morning about three o'clock, and has not ceased yet, and it is now three o'clock Sabbath [Sunday] afternoon. It is expected they will come out over the Neck to-night, and a dreadful battle must ensue." This battle is the one that she watched from Penn's Hill with young John Quincy Adams at her side.

A week later, on June 25, 1775, Abigail finally has collected enough information to give John an accurate report on the battle. What she writes is a military summary of the action, including casualties. It is a long account, but it makes for interesting reading: "Every account agrees in fourteen or fifteen hundred slain and wounded on their side ... When we consider all the circumstances, attending this action, we stand astonished that our people were not all cut off. They had but one hundred feet entrenched, the number who were engaged did not exceed eight hundred, and they with not half ammunition enough; the reinforcements not able to get to them seasonably. The tide was up, and high, so that their [British] floating batteries came upon each side of the causeway, and their row-galleries kept a continual fire. Added to this, the fire from Cops Hill, and from the ships; the town in flames, all around them, and the heat from the flames so intense as scarcely to be borne; the day one of the hottest we have had this season, and the wind blowing smoke in their faces,—only figure to yourself all these circumstances, and then consider that we do not count sixty men lost." This would be the most dramatic account she would write in her letters, but definitely not the last.

By July 25, 1775, she was reporting to John that "Gage has not made any attempts to march out since the battle at Charlestown." She was also noting that "Our army is restless, and wish to be doing something to rid themselves and the land of the vermin and locusts that infest it." This was not her most objective reporting of the war! She also sends on an account she heard from a Captain Vinton of several minor skirmishes. As the months go by, she continues her reports of various British activities, usually in her normal factual style. It would be the following March before the next major action involving the British in Boston would take place. Of course, Abigail did not know this, and her letters report all the alarms and worry the people lived with.

Early March 1776 brought the final confrontation between the British and the patriots in Boston. In a long letter to John, begun on March 2, 1776, Abigail keeps almost a diary of the events of the following five days. On March 4th, she wrote to John with an account of the view and sound of the fighting from Penn's Hill: "I have just returned from Penn's Hill, where I have been sitting to hear the amazing roar of cannon, and from whence I could see every shell which was thrown ... 'Tis now an incessant roar." The next day, Abigail added to her letter a description of the outcome of that fighting: "I hear we got possession of Dorchester Hill last night; four thousand men upon it to-day; lost but one man." Two days later, in her last entry in the letter, Abigail shared her frustration with the results of the fighting: "This day our militia are all returning, without effecting any thing more than taking possession of Dorchester Hill ... I hoped and expected more important and decisive scenes. I would not have suffered all I have for two such hills." In fact, the fighting would flare up again only a few days later, and the British would finally leave Boston in mid-March.

As an historian, Abigail did a good job of writing an interesting account of the events of her day. Looking back, there are times when her information was inaccurate. Her grandson, Charles Francis Adams, in publishing her letters makes notes on those occasions when her information was wrong. For example, in her description of the Battle of Bunker Hill, the casualty figures she reports proved to be incorrect. But for the most part, the overall pictures she presents of the war from a local perspective are what is important. Even though Abigail was often describing the sometimes panicky reactions of the townspeople, when she sat down to write to John, she always seemed to be able to separate out her own fears and provide him with an accurate account. Obviously, Abigail's account covers only a very small part of the American Revolution. But her letters serve as an interesting and fascinating record for people who want an eyewitness account of the experience of people living near Boston during this terrible time.

Chapter 9

SISTER

*I*t is hard for us to imagine how differently from today women lived during the colonial and early American period. We take for granted the freedom women have to choose their own lives, to handle their own money, and to have different opinions from the men in their lives. Women have an independence that Abigail would have found shocking. As part of that independence, women also have a wide circle of women friends who provide a support network for them. Often women are much closer to these friends than they are to their own sisters. In Abigail's time, she corresponded with some women friends, especially with Mercy Otis Warren. But the real support network, the real close women advisors, for Abigail were always her sisters. Her relationship with her sisters was probably no different from that of other sisters at the time. But because the Adamses were famous, all their correspondence was kept, and we are able to go back and see how all women, especially sisters, helped each other and supported each other at that time.

Abigail and her sisters were better educated than other women of their time. Abigail went on to play a unique role as John's wife both in her independence and control of her own life and in her social role as a political leader's wife. Abigail's older sister, Mary Cranch, and her younger sister, Elizabeth Shaw (then Peabody), led more traditional lives. But, like Abigail, they were still strong, independent women who had more influence and power over their lives than most women of their time. All three of the sisters developed real partnerships with their husbands. And the three of them shared each other's triumphs and failures through their lifelong correspondence with each other.

Abigail's older sister, Mary, married John's good friend Richard Cranch in 1762. Mary was twenty-one and Richard was thirty-six at their marriage. Mary and Abigail had always been close to each other and their marrying close friends helped to keep them close. Abigail and John often visited with the Cranches in the early years of their own marriage. When the Cranches moved back to Braintree after having lived in Salem for several years, Mary provided aid and support to Abigail during the long years when John was gone. When Abigail joined John in Europe, it was Mary who took over the care of John's elderly mother. It was also Mary who supervised the Adamses' properties under detailed directions provided by Abigail in her letters. And it was Mary who maintained a close watch on Nabby's suitor, Royall Tyler, while Abigail and Nabby were in Europe. In fact, in the matter of Nabby and Tyler, it was Abigail's and Mary's correspondence that managed to break up the whole relationship. After Abigail became the Vice President's wife, it was Mary to whom she wrote asking that she observe her behavior closely to make sure she didn't become snobbish. Throughout their lives their relationship was a close one and when Mary and Richard both died in 1811, Abigail felt the loss deeply. At the time of their deaths, Abigail was already suffering while watching and caring for Nabby, who was very ill and was going to have surgery, something that was terribly risky in those days. But losing Mary meant she had lost one of her closest friends and would not have her help as she watched Nabby slowly die over the next two years.

Abigail was not as close to her younger sister, Elizabeth, as she was to Mary, but theirs was still a strong, supportive relationship. Elizabeth married later than her sisters did, joking when she turned twenty-four about her lack of suitors. Finally, at the age of twenty-seven she married William Shaw, a school teacher and minister who was boarding at the Smith home in Weymouth. He was only a few years older than Elizabeth, which was somewhat unusual at a time when most girls married men several years older than they. Abigail would always say that Elizabeth was the best writer and the best educated of the three of them. She was the one most suited to having a successful intellectual life. But Elizabeth's life would prove to be a hard one as she struggled financially even to survive. Elizabeth and William Smith moved to a parsonage in Haverhill after their marriage, quite a long way away from her sisters. Elizabeth very much enjoyed her new life as a minister's wife and the intellectual challenges she shared with her husband. They opened a school to prepare boys for entrance into Harvard. All three of Abigail's sons would study with the Shaws. John Quincy would write about what a peaceful and happy home it was. All three of them would always speak of their aunt with real affection. They would remember her help with schoolwork, her praise, and her positive support for everything they did. The three Adams sons would find the Shaw house a refuge from some of the demands made on them by their parents.

Unlike the correspondence with Mary, that between Abigail and Elizabeth shows that they disagreed on many matters. Elizabeth seemed jealous of Abigail's success and her worldly station. Unlike Mary, Elizabeth did feel that Abigail was becoming a snob. Elizabeth also seemed jealous of how close Abigail and Mary were. At one point she invited Mary to visit, telling her she wanted to see her before Abigail returned from England since she knew that once Abigail returned she wouldn't get to see Mary for at least a year. Elizabeth always spoke her mind in her letters, and her correspondence with Abigail is the most human and alive of Abigail's correspondence. There is real affection here but also sisterly squabbling and competition.

But the squabbles were only in the good times. When one needed the others' support and help, the sisters came together. Elizabeth was the one who often needed her sisters' help. William died in September 1794 at age forty-five as a result of his drinking, leaving her with young children and no money. She managed to survive financially. She took in boarders to raise money. She collected the money owed her husband, which he had let go uncollected. Abigail came to her sister's aid, arranging a job for Elizabeth's oldest son so that he could earn money to go to Harvard. Elizabeth surprised both her sisters by deciding to marry again only a year after William's death. She married Stephen Peabody, a widower whom she had known for over twenty-five years. He had been a student boarder at her home in Weymouth and had once been a suitor in her youth. She helped him run a school in Atkinson that had eighty students, and she taught writing as one of the teachers. It seemed that at last she was doing well enough and her sisters could stop worrying about her.

One other part of the relationship among the sisters also deserves some study. All three of them cooperated in raising each other's children. Abigail's three sons found in Elizabeth another mother, less demanding and strict than their own. Elizabeth's son, who needed a stricter environment, was sent to Abigail, who managed to help him get his life in order. Nabby used her Aunt Mary as her confidante and Mary's daughter picked her Aunt Abigail as hers. The sisters among themselves shared in the development of all of their children, giving them a nurturing environment suited to their different needs. It shows the level of their trust and respect for each other that they could recognize their own strengths and weaknesses as mothers and share their duties by helping to raise each other's children.

This relationship among these three women was probably in no way different from the sharing cooperation necessary between other sisters of the time. But this one is remembered all because of whom Abigail married and her fame as his partner.

Chapter 10

CORRESPONDENT

*O*ver 2000 letters written by Abigail Adams still survive. Abigail's grandson, Charles Francis Adams, collected many of her letters and John's letters for publication in 1840. In doing so he decided to destroy many of them that he felt were not important. He also made corrections to her spelling, which, as she feared, really was quite bad. But even with most of her letters missing, the ones that survive are what give us such an interesting picture of Abigail and the times in which she lived.

Abigail herself did not want her letters kept. She always felt her writing was inferior. John always copied over what he wrote into a letterbook so he would have a record of all his correspondence. He wrote to Abigail in 1774, telling her she should do the same. He seemed to realize from the very start that this whole historical event that he was part of should be recorded by the people involved. He knew historians would want to go back and read these letters.

Abigail not only did not keep copies of her letters, but she tried to convince people who received them to destroy the originals. She told her daughter Nabby (in a letter!) that her letters were "trash." John did not agree. He wrote to her on February 4, 1794, while he

This reproduction of Abigail's writing desk sits in the parlor of the Braintree house. Here she would have sat to write her long letters to John while he was away. Notice the Benjamin Blyth portrait above the desk. (Photo by W. Michael Beller.)

was Vice President: "You apologize for the length of your letters, and I ought to excuse the shortness and emptiness of mine. Yours give me more entertainment than all the speeches I hear. There are more good thoughts, fine strokes, and mother wit in them than I hear in a whole week." Someone reading her letters today cannot help but be happy that so many people did not listen to her and did save the letters.

Abigail wrote to everyone. Most of her letters, of course, were family letters. Her correspondence with John while he was away is the most famous of all her letters. There are also a great number of letters (over 360) surviving of those she wrote to her sisters, Mary Cranch and Elizabeth Shaw Peabody. Because she was so close to her sisters, her comments in these letters are very honest and probably best reflect how she really felt about what was happening in her life. Her letter to Mary Cranch, for example, describing what it was like to live in the not-yet-finished White House was quite critical of the conditions there. But in the same letter she admitted she was officially telling everyone it was lovely. How great it is to be able to go back and see what she was really thinking.

She wrote, of course, to her own children, and her letters to John Quincy are especially famous for their comments and advice on political issues. Her granddaughter Caroline, Nabby's daughter, kept the letters Nabby had given her, which she had received from Abigail, and these were later published. Abigail also wrote extensively to other relatives such as her nieces and nephews and her grandchildren.

But she also had a wide circle of correspondence with others outside of her family group. She and Mercy Otis Warren wrote to each other often. Mercy Warren was famous herself as a very strong supporter of women's rights during the Revolutionary War period.

She started the correspondence with Abigail, and it would continue all their lives. They discussed everything from politics to literature to raising children.

Abigail's correspondence with Thomas Jefferson is some of her most famous. They became close friends while Abigail and John were living in Paris, and Abigail trusted him enough to share her frustration with their lives in England once they got there. This correspondence would continue until the end of her life, although there would be a long break during the time that John and Thomas Jefferson became political enemies. It was Abigail who made the first attempt to bring the two friends back together through her letters to Jefferson. Fortunately, the letters between Thomas Jefferson and both John and Abigail Adams survived and have been published.

Many people of the time were letter writers. At a time when there were no telephones and when travel between places was long and difficult, letters were the only way for people to remain in contact with their friends. But Abigail was famous enough that her letters were kept. Her comments on the events of the day, on the everyday life of the times, and on women and their role in society give us a fantastic picture of what it was like to live then. She talks about those kinds of things that weren't kept in official records—especially women's interests that were mostly ignored in men's letters of the time. She wrote about the day-to-day details of running a house and a farm, the cost of things, the illnesses, the neighborhood. She preserved (especially in her letters to her sisters) the gossip of the time. These are the kinds of things that people studying about that time in our history can only find in a few places. Abigail Adams's letters have become very important to people studying American history during this time period.

In addition to preserving the social history of their

time, Abigail Adams's letters are important for the political commentary she included in them. First in her correspondence with John, and later in her correspondence with John Quincy, she was quite outspoken in expressing important political beliefs. She saw situations clearly and showed great political understanding. She wrote freely in her letters to her husband and son, sharing her analysis of events. These letters give a very clear look at the political happenings of the Revolutionary War period and the time after the war. Of course they are also very biased. Abigail never hid the fact that she thought John was an outstanding leader and deserving of his country's thanks and praise.

Wouldn't Abigail be surprised to find that the letters she called "trash" are now considered to be very important historically for both their social and their political content.

Chapter 11

DIPLOMAT

The date was August 7, 1784. Abigail and Nabby were waiting in London. Abigail had not seen John since November 13, 1779 when he left to negotiate the peace treaty between the new United States and Great Britain. When John left he gave her a beautiful locket with strands of both their hair twisted together inside it. He knew that they might never see each other again. This period was particularly difficult for them, with long, lonely times for Abigail between letters. Before leaving for Europe, John had only been home for four months after a one-and-a-half-year absence. Actually, for the last ten years they had only had short visits together. Finally, today they would be reunited.

Her trip across the ocean had not been a pleasant one. For the first ten days after her departure on June 20th, the seas were choppy and Abigail had terrible seasickness. So did all the other women on board, and she was embarrassed to have to have the male crew take care of her. When the seas calmed, she began to feel better. Immediately she set to work making her cabin rooms clean. The remainder of her month-long voyage was pleasant as she spent her time reading and writing. Upon arriving in London, she found that John

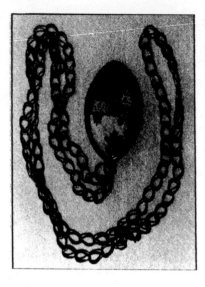

When John left for Europe to serve as a negotiator for the new American nation, he gave Abigail this locket. Inside are pieces of John's and Abigail's hair twisted together. (Courtesy of the U.S. Dept. of the Interior, National Park Service, Adams National Historic Site, Quincy, Massachusetts.)

and John Quincy had left to return to the Netherlands after waiting for her to arrive for over a month. Abigail and Nabby settled in to wait for their return, visiting with many of the former Americans now living in London and seeing the sights of the city. She made it a point to visit the studio of Boston artist John Singleton Copley so she could see the portrait he had painted of John the year before. She wrote to her sister Mary, saying it was a "most beautiful painting" of the husband she had not seen in four and a half years. (July 25, 1784.)

John Quincy arrived to see her on July 30th. For Abigail the reunion with her favorite child was a special time. Her son, just a boy when he had left home at the age of twelve, had grown into a man. Finally, on August 7th, her beloved partner arrived and the long years of waiting ended.

Their first stop was Paris where John was involved in trade negotiations. Abigail and Nabby quickly settled in, enjoying the French theater and society. John was impatient, wanting more than anything to be named United States Ambassador to Great Britain.

As anxious as John was to leave, Abigail would have enjoyed staying in Paris longer. Abigail was enjoying her stay and her lovely home at Auteil, just outside of Paris. Both John and Abigail were enjoying spending time with John Quincy and, more important, having some of the family together again. Abigail wrote to her sister Mary about how pleasant these family times were.

Abigail was shocked at first with the kinds of people she found in Paris. Abigail was a very conservative person. She always dressed plainly and she did not think women should be showy in how they looked. She found the women dancing on stage in theaters shocking. But, over time, she got so used to this that it no longer bothered her.

Abigail was impressed with the educated women she found in France. She became close friends with Madame Lafayette, the wife of the Marquis de Lafayette who had come to help the American Continental Army fight the British during the Revolutionary War.

The Adamses also spent much of their time with Thomas Jefferson and his daughter, Patsy, developing a friendship that both of the Adams and Jefferson would treasure all their lives. The Adamses' stay in Paris was not to be a long one, but Abigail would remember it with pleasure the rest of her life.

In May 1785, John's wish was granted. He was named the first United States Ambassador to Great Britain. John and Abigail made a decision that it was time for John Quincy to go to America to attend Harvard College, which was where John had gone to school. After all the years away from her favorite child, Abigail was losing him again. Now he would be in Massachusetts while she was in England. Abigail wrote to her sisters and asked them to take care of John Quincy and then reluctantly said goodbye to him. Nabby took the loss of John Quincy hard also, and Abigail and Nabby consoled each other as the family planned their move to England. All in all, as much as it was what John wanted, it was a sad time for them.

Serving as the American Ambassador to Great Britain would not be an easy job for John, and Abigail would have to be very careful in everything she said and did. The people of England had always felt their colonies and the people living there to be somehow beneath them in every way. They considered them to be socially inferior. They felt that the colonies lacked the sophistication of the mother country. They were seen as unimportant. The English also saw their former colonies as ungrateful to their motherland. For the English people, to be beaten by these Colonials was a tremendous shock and insult to them.

Now here were John and Abigail coming to England as the first ambassadors from the newly independent colonies. It was a very delicate position to be in. Abigail wrote to Mary that the newspapers were "bursting with envy that an American Minister should be received here with the same marks of attention, politeness, and civility, which are shown to the ministers of any other power." (June 24, 1785.) Everything they would do and say would be watched. They must deal with people who hated them for the country they represented. Worst of all, John knew how important it was to the United States that he win the friendship of England. The colonies had won their independence but they were still weak enough that they needed friendship and trade with the European powers. It was important that John and Abigail get the people of England to like and support them. It was a job at which they could not afford to fail.

John presented his papers and was taken to see the King a week after their arrival in London. Their meeting went well. John was polite but very careful to make it clear he was the ambassador from an equal nation. King George was pleasant and willing "to accept this audience so extraordinary." The London newspapers were not. They began a series of articles insulting the Adamses and letting them know that they considered them to be inferior. For John and Abigail, both of whom were famous for speaking their minds, it was a difficult time. Abigail let out her frustration by writing to Thomas Jefferson about how they were being treated. Thomas Jefferson wrote back about all the terrible things he was hearing said about them in the newspapers. He tried to comfort Abigail and encouraged her to ignore what was being said and help John to ignore it also. Abigail was hurt because the newspapers back home started printing what was in the London papers about them. In her letters to her sisters she complained about their treatment. She worried that friends would believe what they read and turn against them. For Abigail, so used to being a private person and so used to being able to defend herself, it was hard to sit quietly while she and John were being attacked.

While John worked on the political part of being an ambassador, Abigail worked on seeing that the American Ambassador and his family would have the right social setting. She located a home for them to rent and began getting the house and herself ready for the social obligations of an ambassador's family. She prepared herself and Nabby for their presentation to the King and Queen. In everything she did she tried to set what she saw as the right tone for the new American Ambassador. She was the perfect companion to John at this job. She was always aware that she was establishing something new for her country. She was the social diplomat while John was the political diplomat.

Before her presentation to the King and Queen, she thought a long time about the impression she wanted to make. Her image of the America she wanted to present was of a country that was plain but elegant. She would wear nothing fancy, but what she wore was made of the best materials. Her plain but elegant philosophy carried over to the Ambassador's home. Abigail planned every detail to match the image she was building for America. She continued to analyze everything she said and did to make sure her representation of America was perfect. And she continued to demand that everyone treat her and her family with the respect due to them as America's official representatives.

Personally she had very mixed feelings about the English. Her letters to her sisters show her disgust with the Queen's Court and the snobbish rituals of English society. She writes to Elizabeth, "I shall never have much society with this kind of people, for they would not like me any more that I do them." (August 15, 1785.) At the same time, she found herself liking many of the people and sights of her "mother country." She especially enjoyed attending the theater once she got used to the showiness of the female performers. But she remained an American. For the most part, outside of official duties she chose her friends from among the other American women in London or American visitors.

Some of the pleasure of her stay was dampened by the financial problems they faced. Living in London and entertaining at the level of an ambassador was not cheap. As always it was Abigail who was left with the responsibility for their financial survival. A household her size was expected to have at least eleven servants. She cut the need to eight although even then she found the whole system wasteful. For Abigail, who had always been thrifty, it was a difficult and frustrating situation. She wanted to do away with waste and with paying servants who only really worked part of the time. But she also knew that being cheap would make America look cheap and would not be in keeping with the image that she and John were working to give of America as an equal power. Abigail spent much of her time trying to hit the right balance between being thrifty and being miserly.

Abigail's time as a diplomatic figure was a special time for her. For the first time, she was there as John's partner in his political career. Even after their long separation, their partnership came back together well. She was a real help to him, and she was a successful diplomat herself in setting standards for the status of the new nation. They made a perfect couple to be the first diplomatic representatives from America to Great Britain. Living in France and England also gave Abigail some world experience that would help in the next two political positions John would move into—first as Vice President and then as President. Abigail, with her newly developed social skills and cosmopolitan knowledge of how the Europeans did things, was ready to help set the standards for the social life of America's highest offices.

Chapter 12

VICE PRESIDENT'S WIFE

*J*ohn Adams became the first Vice President of the newly formed United States when George Washington was elected President in 1789. For both John and Abigail, along with George and Martha Washington, this would be a time of setting the traditions that would be followed by all later Presidents and Vice Presidents and their wives. All four of the people involved seemed to understand the historical significance of what they were doing.

Abigail was delighted with John's new position. She looked forward to the opportunity to see him act on the national scene. Abigail was always John's strongest supporter. She had long felt that John deserved a role in leading the new country. She felt John had given a lot of himself to help create the new country. If he had not spent all those years at the Continental Congress and serving as a negotiator and then as an ambassador, he would have been a successful lawyer. They would not have had the financial problems they now faced. Abigail felt he was owed the office. She also supported the election of George Washington as President. It was not a question of John being elected President (at least not until after George Washington's term). She and everyone else wanted George Washington as the first President. She shared John's disappointment, though, when he only received thirty-four of the sixty-nine electoral votes. However, when John, with his pride hurt, felt he should turn down the Vice Presidency, she helped him get over his hurt feelings and take the position.

Being Abigail, she was nervous about her own ability not to embarrass John in this new high office. Even now, after all the years and distance from being a small town, uneducated girl from Weymouth, Abigail still worried about whether she would be an acceptable Vice President's wife. But she was excited to be able to try. On the opposite side, she worried that people would think her snobbish because of her new position. Or worse still, that she would begin acting like a snob herself. She asked her sister to watch her behavior and tell her if she thought she was putting on airs.

She was also worried about some of the practical details. How could they afford for her to join John? Who would work the farm? How about the family needs, especially the problems Thomas was having getting settled into a career, which she needed to help him work out? But John made it clear that he wanted her with him this time and gave her instructions on how to take care of the problems.

Abigail closed up the house in Braintree, made arrangements for the care of their farm, and arranged to have their furniture shipped. In June 1789, she left Massachusetts for the capital, which was in New York City at that time, where John was waiting for her. John had found them a house outside of New York on Staten Island called Richmond Hill. Abigail would fall in love with it right away. Although it was not furnished, everything else about it was perfect. The house was exactly what she wanted. It reminded her of all the beautiful manor homes they had seen in Europe. Abigail settled herself in, setting up a household fit for the first Vice President of the United States.

Abigail saw her first task as Vice President's wife as getting to know First Lady Martha Washington and finding out how she could help her with the heavy demands placed upon the First Lady. She called on Martha the day after she arrived in New York. She and Martha became good friends right from the start. The Adamses and Washingtons began to spend a lot of time socializing together, and not just at the public activities that both couples had to attend. The two couples enjoyed meeting for dinner and conversation. Abigail wrote to her sister Mary about how much she was enjoying her friendship with Martha Washington. She said that the two of them spent hours discussing their grandchildren and telling family stories.

Abigail seemed to enjoy her new role and place in the social order. She worked out with Martha and the wives of other government leaders a system of receptions rotating through their houses so that no one person would have to do all of the entertaining. She selected Monday evenings for hers after Martha had made her selection of Friday. Other wives took the other evenings of the week. She also gave a weekly dinner for twenty-four people at Richmond Hill. All the entertaining reminded Abigail of how much she had enjoyed the social life of Europe. And she realized how much she had missed it during her year back in Braintree before John became Vice President.

John was not adjusting to his new position as easily as Abigail was to hers. During the time after he became Vice President, while Abigail was in Massachusetts, he wrote to Abigail about the job of Vice President. His words would become the most famous description of the office: "My country has in its wisdom contrived for me the most insignificant office that ever the invention of man contrived or his imagination conceived." (December 9, 1793.) His feelings about the job did not improve over time. John found himself in the center of the petty politics of the men in the government.

Worse still, he found himself in a position where he could do little to change things. His job was to preside over the Senate, and his opinion was not really needed unless there was a tie vote on an issue. John, who had never been particularly patient, found his inability to change things to be very frustrating. He found himself lecturing to members of the House and Senate on what he thought were the proper ways they should treat President Washington. They laughed at him and nicknamed him "His Rotundity." The more he lectured them, the more they ignored him or became angry with him. He was accused of trying to establish an American monarchy and of trying to make the presidency stronger so that he would have more power when he became president.

As time went on, two different views of how the federal government should develop were argued back and forth among the people serving Washington. John became a very strong advocate for the federalists, as they were called. His old friend Thomas Jefferson became a strong advocate of the anti-federalists. The federalists wanted a stronger central government than the anti-federalists did. The federalists saw the need for a very powerful President. The anti-federalists wanted more checks upon the power of the President and a more powerful Congress. The dispute was straining the long friendship between John Adams and Thomas Jefferson. While Abigail might find being the Vice President's wife a great social role, John was finding the Vice Presidency to be a most unpleasant political role.

The new capital did not stay in New York. It was

moved to Philadelphia in 1790. John went ahead and rented them a house and Abigail was left to pack everything up once again for a move in November 1790. Their new home at Bush Hill outside of Philadelphia became an active part of the Philadelphia social scene. Abigail found herself at the theater, teas, balls, parties, and receptions six afternoons and evenings each week. She welcomed a visit home to Braintree in May 1791 to rest and recuperate before returning to yet another home in Philadelphia itself in October. All the socializing made Abigail ill, and when she and John returned to Braintree for the summer of 1792, she decided to stay there and have him return to Philadelphia alone in the fall. From her home in Quincy (part of Braintree had split off to become a separate town the year before), she again kept in touch with John through letters.

John was left alone to face the brutal political attacks of the 1792 election campaign. At home, Abigail, ill again, became upset by all the terrible things that were being said about John. The words had no real effect on the election though, and John was reelected to the Vice Presidency with 77 of the 127 votes.

Now John and Abigail faced the financial question again. They had lost a lot of money during John's first term as Vice President because of the low salary and the entertaining that Abigail had to do. The entertaining had also been exhausting for Abigail. They made a decision to have Abigail stay in Quincy. John would live in a rented home in Philadelphia and come home to Quincy for the summers. Abigail would go back to being a "farmeress," and their famous correspondence would continue again. After ten years together most of the time, the duties of the partnership would be divided again.

The political turmoil in Philadelphia continued over John's second term as Vice President as it had over his first. In Abigail's letters he found his refuge from the mean-spiritedness of the political scene. John had promised Abigail that after his second term as Vice President he would have had enough of politics. He was planning to come home to Quincy and resume his farming and be a "private man." Abigail, knowing John so well, would not be surprised when three years later John began to change his mind. On January 7, 1796, he wrote to Abigail, saying, "The probability is strong that I shall make a voluntary retreat, and spend the rest of my days in a very humble style, with you." Two weeks later, on January 20th, he was claiming "A pious and a philosophical resignation to the voice of the people in this case." By February, he was acknowledging to Abigail how much he would miss being part of the government if he were not elected President.

Abigail would also not be surprised at the attacks that were made on John when he let people know he was willing to be President. She wrote to her son Thomas about the "false and glaring absurdities" that people were using to "deceive and delude the people." (November 7, 1796.) On February 8, 1797 John announced that he had received seventy-one votes in the Electoral College and was "President by three votes" of the United States. Thomas Jefferson was Vice President. For Abigail, her peaceful time in Quincy was over and she would become part of the whirlwind again.

Chapter 13

FIRST LADY

*O*ne of the most lasting images of early American history is the one of Abigail Adams hanging her laundry to dry in the unfinished East Room of the White House. However, this picture represents only a very small part of Abigail's life as First Lady. John Adams became President on March 4, 1797. The Adamses did not move into the President's House (now known as the White House) until late in 1800 at the very end of Adams's presidency.

John Adams went to his inauguration alone. No members of his family were in Philadelphia to go with him. Abigail had stayed in Quincy to be with John's mother, who was dying. It was a very simple inaugural ceremony and John wrote to Abigail that he did not decide until the last minute whether he should give a speech. In the end he decided to ask for unity and that the dissension between the political parties come to an end. John felt that American government was divided right then between two extreme positions. He felt that the divisions between the federalists and the anti-federalists was damaging the new nation. He felt that America was also divided between supporting France or England. In both domestic and foreign affairs John would try to hit a middle ground between the extremes.

Because Abigail was not with John, we have a record of what she was thinking about as he was about to become President. She wrote to him on February 8, 1797, "My thoughts and my meditations are with you, though personally absent. My feelings ... are solemnized by a sense of the obligations, the important trusts, and numerous duties." Then she wrote of her prayer "That you may be enabled to discharge them with honor to yourself, with justice and impartiality to your country, and with satisfaction to this great people."

Knowing he would need her support, Abigail hurried to Philadelphia to join John. She wrote to John on April 26, 1797, telling him that with his mother's funeral over, she was ready to join him: "I want no courting to come. I am ready and willing to follow my husband wherever he chooses." She slipped quickly into her role as First Lady, spending long days entertaining. Abigail knew that her husband's presidency would not be an easy one. In replying to a letter from her friend, Mercy Warren, on March 4, 1797, the day of John's inauguration, she thanked her for her congratulations to them on John's election. But she wrote also that this "unsolicited gift of a free and enlightened people ... calls for every exertion of the head and every virtue of the heart to do justice to so sacred a trust." She acknowledged right from the beginning that "offences will come" and that she hoped when it was all over to "retire esteemed, beloved and equally respected with my predecessor." Neither John nor Abigail would retire with that esteem. Their fears of the difficult times ahead were fully justified.

Abigail and John moved into the house that the Washingtons had lived in on Market Street in Philadelphia. In a delightfully domestic letter to her sister

Mary, Abigail preserved a picture of what it was like to be First Lady at this time. She talked about having to get up at five o'clock in the morning just to have any time to get personal things done before her day as First Lady began. She spoke in her letters about all the social activities she had to attend. She also complained to Mary about all of the expenses of entertaining as President and First Lady. Unlike the Washingtons, who were wealthy, the Adamses had to manage to live on John's $14,000 a year salary. For the remainder of John's Presidency, her letters to her sisters and others would often contain complaints about money.

Over the four years of John's Presidency, Abigail would suffer greatly from the attacks in the newspapers on John's policies and on their personal lives. Abigail was referred to as "Her Majesty." She was accused of being cheap, but also of spending too much money. John was attacked for his policies as well as for his impatience. The attacks were often personal and nasty. Abigail would wait until well after they retired to Quincy to tell her friend, Mercy Warren, of how those attacks had affected her. She wrote of being afraid to write to anyone for fear of being misquoted. She complained that "The most innocent expressions have been twisted, mangled, and tortured into meanings wholly foreign to the sentiments of the writer." (January 16, 1803.)

Despite John's efforts to keep a balance between the two views warring in the government, the divisions in the country became more obvious. For Abigail there was personal pain that political divisions were causing a break in the long friendship both the Adamses had shared with Thomas Jefferson. Abigail felt personally betrayed by Jefferson as the two men grew further and further apart.

Abigail would also suffer for the closeness of her

relationship with her husband. The hostile press would continually accuse her of having power over her husband's decisions. Many of her biographers make it clear that she did serve as a consultant to her husband and that she did usually know things before they were released to the general public. For the people who wished to find fault with her, this was evidence of undue influence over John. But for anyone who takes the time to study her life carefully, this was just a continuation of the partnership that John and Abigail had forged so many years before as they worked the farm in the quiet, early years of their marriage. After all these years of marriage, John still found Abigail to be his sounding board and his discussion partner, and he still turned to her when he needed to refine his thoughts on an issue.

Halfway through his Presidency, John and Abigail returned home to Quincy for a summer vacation. Along the way Abigail became so sick that people felt sure that she was dying. She finally recovered after being deathly ill for over eleven weeks. There was no way that Abigail could return to Philadelphia with John for the winter months that year. After John left and their correspondence began yet again, Abigail joked about being only "a half way politician," a recognition of how much John counted on her advice. As the winter wore on, John came under attack yet again, this time because Abigail was NOT giving him advice. Critics of his policies said they were the result of not having Abigail there to advise him. John, who recognized how funny the criticism was, wrote to Abigail, "O!, how they lament Mrs. Adams absence! She is a good counsellor!" (February 25, 1799.) Both John and Abigail must have enjoyed this change in viewpoint and appreciated its irony.

Abigail felt well enough to return to Philadelphia for the following winter. She was actually feeling better than she had in years and she settled back into her First Lady role with great enthusiasm. John had also settled into his role as President by now and even began to look forward to possibly being elected to a second term. Abigail was torn between wanting to go home to Quincy and knowing that if John felt his country needed him, he was bound to be "obedient to her voice." As the election came closer and the political attacks grew stronger, John and Abigail began to face the very likely possibility that he would not be reelected. They began to make plans for their retirement.

As their annual summer time in Quincy ended in 1800, John and Abigail prepared to move into the President's House in the new capital of Washington, D.C. John went first and Abigail followed later. She stopped along the way to see her son Charles, dying in New York City as a result of his drinking. Abigail finally reached Washington on November 16th (she had gotten lost between Baltimore and the new capital).

The President's House was far from the White House we think of today. Abigail found an unfinished building without furnishings. Even the stairways to the second floor were not in. Yet, she could see in it the building it would become, writing to her daughter on November 21, 1800, "It is a beautiful spot, capable of every improvement." She could also note the things it lacked: "There is not a single apartment finished ... We have not the least fence, yard, or other convenience ... The great, unfinished audience room I make a drying-room of, to hang up the clothes in. The principal stairs are not up, and will not be this winter." But given the election results, she would not be living in the unfinished mansion for very long. Only three months after they moved into the building, it was time for them to leave so that Thomas Jefferson, the new President, could move in.

If you visit the White House today you can see John Adams's famous prayer, written to Abigail on the first night he stayed in the President's House. It is carved on the mantel in the State Dining Room: "I pray heaven to bestow the best of Blessings on this House and all that shall hereafter inhabit it. May none but honest and wise men ever rule under this roof."

Chapter 14

PRESIDENT'S MOTHER

*A*bigail Adams would have been famous simply as the wife of the first Vice President and second President of the United States. She would have been famous for her role in her husband's career and the unique partnership they forged. But what gives her a one-of-a-kind status is the fact that she is the only presidential wife in our history who was also the mother of a president. John Quincy Adams's success came from several different factors. Some of his success resulted from the experience he gained in his teens when he served as his father's secretary. Some came from the political connections that allowed him to rise in government office. But a great deal of it came from Abigail.

Abigail believed strongly in the need for education of women. She felt that this was a critical need since she saw that one of the most important roles that a woman had was to be the educator of her children, particularly of her sons. From the time John Quincy Adams (called Johnny) was small, she worked at the job of educating her son. From the poetry she taught him when he was only three years old, to the efforts she made to read and discuss books with him at a young age, to her efforts to acquaint him with the people and the events of

This painting of John Quincy Adams was done when he was fifteen years old. Remarkably, he was serving as secretary to the American Minister to Russia. (Courtesy of the U.S. Dept. of the Interior, National Park Service, Adams National Historic Site, Quincy, Massachusetts.)

the American Revolution — in everything she did for John Quincy, Abigail worked to prepare him for his future.

John Quincy sought and listened to his parents' advice in all career matters. He had been appointed by George Washington as minister to the Netherlands in 1794, and then as minister to Portugal in 1796. George Washington described him in 1797 as the most valuable minister he had abroad and recommended that John not let the fact that John Quincy was his son stop him from continuing to utilize his services, and even to promote him. John followed that advice when he needed someone of John Quincy's experience and ability to serve as minister to Prussia (what is now Germany). The result was a vicious attack on John by the press, who accused him of trying to start a hereditary monarchy and of giving his son an allowance from the U.S. Treasury. Abigail did not take the criticism of her husband and her son well. She knew that John Quincy was the best person for the job and knew that John needed his services.

The only area in which John Quincy maintained a stubborn independence from his parents was in his marriage to Louisa Catherine Johnson in London in July 1797. He had met her once many years before when she was a young child, and he met her again in 1795 through her father, who was American Consul in London. They developed an instant liking for each other. John and Abigail were not happy with the relationship, but with the distance between them and letters taking so long to go back and forth, they could have little effect on the developing romance. What did almost destroy the relationship was the failure of Louisa's father's business interests. John Quincy's rather unsympathetic comments aroused Louisa's anger. At the same time, Louisa's father began to press for their marriage, knowing that John Quincy was a "good" match for his daughter; better than she could find now that he was no longer wealthy. John and Abigail could only watch the developing situation from a distance and advise their son to be patient and cautious in selecting a marriage partner. Ironically, John Quincy was hesitating for financial reasons, and it was his father's appointment of him as minister to Prussia that gave him the security he needed. Eight days after hearing of his appointment, he married Louisa on July 26, 1797. Abigail did not learn of his marriage until she read about it in the newspaper on November 2nd. His letter telling her that he had married had not yet arrived.

John ordered the recall of John Quincy from Prussia before leaving office as President so that he would not have the humiliation of having him removed by his enemy and successor, Thomas Jefferson. Abigail wrote and counseled him to prepare himself and Louisa carefully for their homecoming, as the press would be looking to attack them. They finally arrived home in September 1801. John Quincy headed to Quincy to see his parents, whom he had not seen in seven years; Louisa headed to Washington to see hers. In December John Quincy finally brought her home to meet his parents. John liked Louisa immediately, but the visit did not go well between Abigail and Louisa. Abigail liked Louisa but found her to be lacking in her support of John Quincy and his career. For Abigail, who had been John's strongest supporter, this was something that she saw as a great fault in a wife.

Although John Quincy had been away from home for seven years and had his own family, Abigail continued to involve herself in directing his career. John Quincy appreciated her involvement and opinions. Perhaps Abigail felt that she needed to continue her direction because Louisa was not as supportive a partner as she felt John Quincy deserved. For whatever reason, John Quincy continued to consult with both his parents on his career decisions.

Abigail was delighted with John Quincy's election to the United States Senate in 1803. She began a correspondence with him that is very similar in tone to her earlier correspondence with John. She served as an honest critic, supporting and reinforcing his successes, and helping him to refine his political thinking. She even took him to task for being neglectful of his clothes. John Quincy in turn kept her up-to-date on what was happening in Washington and listened to her astute political commentary. As he found himself increasingly taking political stands that alienated many members of his own party, he depended on both his parents' comments to support him in his stands. Abigail, in a most understanding letter, praised his moral strength in standing up for his beliefs and offered her prayer that he would always "hold fast in your integrity." No one could have had more supportive backing than John Quincy received from his mother.

In 1809, John Quincy received some recognition from President Madison with his appointment as Minister to Russia. Abigail, although proud of her son, knew she was ill and felt she was probably saying goodbye to him for the last time. She again corresponded with him but also worked on the home front to get her son an appointment in the United States. When John Quincy was appointed an Associate Justice of the Supreme Court, she was delighted that he would be returning home. But John Quincy refused the appointment, preferring to remain in his position in Russia. He would not be home for quite some time, since he ended up serving as ambassador and chief negotiator for American interests on a number of occasions, including the negotiation of the peace treaty ending the

War of 1812. Abigail was particularly proud of his appointment as Minister to Great Britain, the post his father had held, and she shared her memories of London with Louisa in her letters. Finally, in November 1816, John Quincy was called home to become Secretary of State. Abigail was ecstatic. On August 18, 1817, John Quincy and his family finally came back home. They had a joyful month's reunion before John Quincy left for Washington. The following summer they visited again. It would be Abigail's last visit with her son.

She would not live to see John Quincy become President. But her guidance and her constant support of his career were major forces behind his achievement of that position. How proud she would have been.

Chapter 15

GRANDMOTHER

*A*bigail Adams found being a grandmother a more relaxing experience than being a mother. She very much enjoyed her seventeen grandchildren. She would be able to guide their educations as she had the educations of her own children. She would also have more of an opportunity to enjoy and play with her grandchildren than she ever did with her own children. Several of them would even live with her for various periods of time while they were growing up.

Abigail's daughter, Nabby, married Colonel William Smith while the family was in London. Nabby had three sons and a daughter — William, John, Thomas (who died as an infant), and Caroline. Caroline was Abigail's favorite grandchild. Her letters to Caroline openly show her affection, unlike some of her more formal earlier letters to her own children. On February 26, 1811, she responded to a letter from Caroline with news of the snow in Massachusetts and of the health of her dog, Miss Juno. She opened the letter with the words, "Your letter, my dear Caroline, gave me pleasure." She closes her letter with these fond words: "Adieu, my dear ... Most affectionately, Your Grandmother, Abigail Adams."

John Quincy and his wife, Louisa Catherine Johnson, had four children — George Washington, John, Charles Francis, and Louisa Catherine (who died when only thirteen months old, while the family was in Russia). When John Quincy went to Russia to serve as ambassador in 1809, he and Louisa left George, eight years old, and John, six years old, in the care of their grandparents at Quincy. George and John would remain with them until 1815 when their father, John Quincy, was named ambassador to Great Britain, and they joined their parents and younger brother in England. It was Abigail's grandson, Charles Francis Adams, who would collect her letters and publish them in 1848, and would also collect and publish the works of his grandfather.

Charles, who married Sally Smith, the sister of Nabby's husband, William Smith, had two children, Susanna and Abby. Charles died from alcoholism in 1800. Abigail had visited with him for the last time on her way down to the new President's House in Washington in November of that year. His two children and their mother remained close to Abigail and John, often visiting them at Quincy for long periods of time after they retired. In fact, it was Abigail's granddaughter Susanna who accompanied her on the long trip home to Quincy after John was not reelected to the presidency. John stayed behind for Thomas Jefferson's inauguration.

Thomas Boylston was the last of the children of John and Abigail to marry, and also the oldest when he married. He married Ann (Nancy) Harrod, to Abigail's delight, in 1805. Abigail had been encouraging the two to marry for some time, as she was very close to Nancy. They had seven children, four sons and three daughters (one of whom died as an infant). The oldest son, Thomas Boylston, died young while serving in the

Jane Stuart made this copy of her father's painting of Abigail, done after the Adamses retired to Quincy. It hangs in the Long Room of the Adams Mansion. (Courtesy of the U.S. Dept. of the Interior, National Park Service, Adams National Historic Site, Quincy, Massachusetts.)

The companion portrait of John Adams by Jane Stuart. (Courtesy of the U.S. Dept. of the Interior, National Park Service, Adams National Historic Site, Quincy, Massachusetts.)

army. Two other sons, John Quincy II and Joseph Harrod, died while on duty in the navy. The youngest son, Isaac Hull, was expelled from West Point and did very little with his life after that. Of the two living daughters, Abigail, who was an artist, also died young. Lizzie (Elizabeth Coombs), who lived until 1903 in Massachusetts, never married. Because Thomas married so late, these children of Thomas and Nancy are the least well known of the Adamses' grandchildren. Also, Thomas and his wife may have had the largest family, but they had no grandchildren of their own since none of their children ever had children themselves.

For Abigail, her time with her grandchildren was very pleasurable to her. However, being Abigail, she remained always an educator, molding her grandchildren as she had molded her children. She lectured to her sister in a letter on June 5, 1809 that "It behooves us, who are parents or grandparents, to give our daughters and granddaughters, when their education devolves upon us, such an education as shall qualify them for the useful and domestic duties of life, that they should learn the proper use and improvement of time, since 'time was given for use, not waste.'"

Writing to her grandchildren, she would share what wisdom she felt she had acquired over her long life. On October 26, 1814, the day after her fiftieth wedding anniversary, she wrote to her granddaughter, Caroline: "Yesterday completes a half century since I entered the married state, then just your age. I have great cause for thankfulness, that I have lived so long, and enjoyed so large a portion of happiness as has been my lot. The greatest source of unhappiness I have known in that period has arisen from the long and cruel separations, which I was called, in a time of war and with a young family around me, to submit to." On her sixty-eighth birthday, Abigail wrote a long letter to Caroline, in which she evaluates her life and her actions over the years and then offers to Caroline a summary of her philosophy of life: "What have I done for myself or others in this long period of my sojourn, that I can look back upon with pleasure, or reflect upon with approbation? Many, very many follies and errors of judgment and conduct rise up before me, and ask forgiveness of that Being, who seeth into the secret recesses of the heart, and from whom nothing is hidden. I think I may with truth say, that in no period of my life have the vile passions had control over me. I bear no enmity to any human being ... I am one of those who are willing to rejoice always. My disposition and habits are not of the gloomy kind." (November 19-27, 1812.)

Abigail would live long enough to see four of her great-grandchildren, a very unusual accomplishment in that time of shorter life spans. To the end she would continue to have her grandchildren around her and enjoy counseling them and guiding their lives. Charles Francis Adams, closing out his memoir of his grandmother's life, which opens his collection of her letters, provided a fitting memorial to his grandmother: "It was the fortune of the Editor to know the subject of his Memoir only during the last year of her life [he had been in Russia and England with his parents for most of his life], and when he was too young fully to comprehend the worth of her character; but it will be a source of unceasing gratification to him, that he had been permitted to pay this tribute, however inadequate, to her memory."

Chapter 16

PEACEMAKER

*W*hen one looks back on the time of the Revolutionary War, two great names come to mind as the persons who were most responsible for the ideas that served as the basis for our new country. These two men are John Adams and Thomas Jefferson. For a time they were the best of friends. Then their political differences led them to become enemies during the time each of them served as President. Both of them were proud men, each convinced of the rightness of his opinions. Abigail Adams was caught between them in their disagreement. It was against her nature to disagree with her partner in anything in his public life. But she had become a close friend of Thomas Jefferson during the time John Adams and Thomas Jefferson were serving in France. It would be Abigail who, without telling John, would try to mend the break between the two men. Abigail, who usually was so stubborn and unforgiving in her own friendships, would become for once a peacemaker.

Fifty-one letters between Abigail Adams and Thomas Jefferson still exist. Many, many more were lost. Most of the letters are from the time when John Adams was serving as Ambassador to England. When Abigail first arrived in Europe, she and John spent nine months in Paris before he was assigned to London. During that time, Thomas Jefferson was almost a member of their family. They spent a great deal of time with him and his daughter, and Abigail enjoyed their conversations together. All four members of the Adams family in France enjoyed his company. Abigail, in writing to Jefferson upon their arrival in London, told him how they were all sorry to be leaving "the only person with whom my Companion could associate with perfect freedom, and unreserve." (June 6, 1785.)

When Abigail and John arrived in London, both of them began an extensive correspondence with Thomas Jefferson. The letters among the three show a strong understanding of the delicate negotiations going on to ensure that their new country was treated with the respect a sovereign power deserved. They quoted newspaper accounts back and forth and analyzed their meaning and effect. The letters also reflect the close friendship among the three.

Abigail, in her first letter, felt she must "apoligize for thus freely scribling to you." (June 6, 1785.) Thomas Jefferson writes back with, "thanks for your condescension in having taken the first step for settling a correspondence which I so much desired." (June 21, 1785.) From then on their correspondence never faltered during both their stays in Europe. They discussed politics, theater, literature, and mutual friends. They ran errands for each other, sending needed goods back and forth between the two countries. Thomas Jefferson also felt he could ask her questions about social decisions that he felt he and John might not be sensitive enough to deal with. At times when John was too busy to write, Abigail also delivered his political messages to Thomas Jefferson. Later, when Jefferson's other daughter arrived in London on her way to join her father in France, it was Abigail to whom Thomas Jefferson entrusted her care.

What is most amazing in reading the letters is the equal nature of their friendship. Abigail, in writing to Thomas Jefferson, sounded very much as she did in writing to John. She offered her usual outspoken political commentary: "In this Country there is a great want of many French comodities, Good Sense, Good Nature, Political Wisdom and benevolence." (November 24, 1785.) She shared family news. When she had been asked to purchase something for him, she advised him on choosing the right item at a thrifty price. The tone of the letters was often light and informal and even humorous. When Abigail was too busy to write, Thomas Jefferson would teasingly complain to John, asking him to have Abigail write, claiming she had not written to him in a "hundred years." The return of the Adamses to Massachusetts in 1788 would end the correspondence between Abigail and Thomas Jefferson. Their next letter would be sixteen years later in 1804.

During the intervening years, John Adams had been Vice President and then President, with Thomas Jefferson serving as Vice President. Their political differences had caused the friendship to end. For three and a half years, Abigail and Thomas Jefferson had not even spoken to each other. Then Thomas Jefferson's daughter died. This was the daughter whom Abigail had cared for when she had arrived in London at age eight, frightened and homesick. The deep feeling Abigail had for Polly Jefferson allowed her to write to her former friend and now enemy. Her letter to Thomas Jefferson on May 20, 1804, is a beautiful and moving one sharing her own sorrow and offering him support and sympathy. She signed the letter as one "who once took pleasure in subscribing Herself Your Friend." Her letter gave Thomas Jefferson the opportunity in his reply on June 13th to "regret that circumstances should have arisen which have seemed to draw a line of separation between us," and to open with her a discussion about his break with John and his desire to mend the broken friendship. He told Abigail that "the friendship with which you honoured me has ever been valued, and fully reciprocated."

The seven letters between them at this time provide an opportunity to hear Thomas Jefferson and Abigail justify the different political decisions made by the Adams and Jefferson Administrations. They discussed the political differences between John Adams and Thomas Jefferson openly, discussed the hurt resulting from some of the official actions each had taken, and defended their own positions. They reopened the lines of communication between them, but never quite got to the point of mending their friendship. Finally, Abigail ended the correspondence between them. A month later she gave the entire correspondence to John to read. John did not comment upon it but copied it over into his own letter book, noting that he never knew it was taking place.

The friendship was not healed immediately, but Abigail had planted the seed that would allow a correspondence between Thomas Jefferson and John to begin again once both of them retired from the public arena. Eight years after she and Thomas Jefferson exchanged letters, Benjamin Rush, a friend of both Thomas Jefferson and John Adams, sent a mutual friend on a visit to the Adamses in Massachusetts. The visit went well and Benjamin Rush began strongly encouraging both sides to mend their friendship. It was John who took the first step, sending Thomas Jefferson some cloth produced in Massachusetts and acting in his letter as if nothing had ever disturbed their friendship. Thomas Jefferson responded the same way, calling to mind their days of friendship. Thus resumed the correspondence between the two greatest minds of the Revolutionary War period, a correspondence that would continue this time until they died within a few hours of each other on July 4, 1826.

It was Abigail who took the first step in resuming her own correspondence with Thomas Jefferson by adding a note to the end of one of John's letters to Jefferson in July 1813, sending "the regards of an old friend, which are still cherished and preserved through all the changes and v[ic]issitudes which have taken place since we first became acquainted." Thomas Jefferson jumped at the opportunity to write back. Their letters continued off and on until Abigail's death in October 1818, with both of them often recalling the pleasant days they remembered together in Paris.

This photograph of the Adams Mansion shows the kitchen wing that Abigail had added to the back of the house to make it into a year-round home. On the right side of the house is the other wing, which she added as a surprise for John. It had the "Long Room" on the first floor and a study for John on the second floor. (Courtesy of the U.S. Dept. of the Interior, National Park Service, Adams National Historic Site, Quincy, Massachusetts.)

Chapter 17

RETIRED

*W*hen John and Abigail retired to Quincy in March 1801, it was for a well deserved rest. Now, after all their separations over the years, they would remain in one place together until Abigail's death. When Abigail learned that John would not be elected to a second term as President, she wrote to her son Thomas, "At my age, and with my bodily infirmities, I shall be happier at Quincy. Neither my habits, nor my education or inclinations have led me to an expensive style of living, so that on that score I have little to mourn over. If I did not rise with dignity, I can at least fall with ease, which is the more difficult task." (November 13, 1800.)

Even in retirement, Abigail stayed involved in the world around her. Her letters became even more numerous. She served as advisor to John Quincy in detailed correspondence with him. She wrote constantly to family members and became actively involved in her grandchildren's lives. She became once again a farmeress, managing the land at their home in Quincy. After all the years of her management, it is no surprise that John did not bother trying to take over running their lands. She continued her upgrading of the home they had purchased in 1787 after returning from Europe.

This house, now called the Adams Mansion, is the one that John and Abigail bought while still in London. It is located in Quincy, Massachusetts. Abigail had her sister Mary Cranch supervise all the repairs and preparations to get the house ready for their return. This painting of the house was done in 1798 by E. Malcolm. (Courtesy of the U.S. Dept. of the Interior, National Park Service, Adams National Historic Site, Quincy, Massachusetts.)

She had already added a kitchen wing with a bedroom above it so that it could become a year-round home. In 1798 she had surprised John with the addition of a whole new section on the house, which included a large library/office for him on the second floor. She took great care in arranging this project.

Their retirement home, which became the home of four generations of Adamses, was large enough to allow some of their children and grandchildren to live with them. Sally Adams, the widow of Charles, and her two daughters visited often. John Quincy's two sons lived with them while he served as an ambassador from 1809 until his return six years later. Nabby spent time here with her mother during the last few years of her life as her illness became worse.

John settled into his retirement with great joy. He spent his mornings working on writing his autobiography. Abigail said in her letters that she was busier than ever, telling the friends and relatives she wrote to about how hard it was for her even to find time to write with her grandchildren playing noisily in her room.

A visitor to Quincy today can capture the feeling of what it must have been like for the Adamses in their sunny home in those last years of Abigail's life. Abigail's lilacs still grow in the front of the house. The "long room," their formal parlor that was part of Abigail's surprise addition for John, is furnished with the chairs and couch that John purchased for them in Europe. The room is set up as they might have had it, with the firescreens next to the special ladies' chairs near the fireplace to protect their faces from the heat of the fire. In the hall, the visitor can stop to look in Abigail's ornate mirror. Up the stairs is one of Abigail's dresses, carefully preserved in a large dresser. The dresser has its own story—it, along with other pieces of furniture, was damaged in an overseas move, and Abigail wrote

The Long Room in the new wing of the house was furnished with the chairs and couch that John bought while he was in Europe. This furniture was also used by the Adamses in the Oval Room of the White House during the short time they lived there. (Courtesy of the U.S. Dept. of the Interior, National Park Service, Adams National Historic Site, Quincy, Massachusetts.)

Next to the fireplace in the Long Room are two ladies' chairs, specially designed for ladies to sit in with their wide skirts. Next to each chair is a firescreen to protect the faces of the women from the heat of the fire. (Courtesy of the U.S. Dept. of the Interior, National Park Service, Adams National Historic Site, Quincy, Massachusetts.)

This is the bedroom where John and Abigail slept in the Adams Mansion. Around the fireplace are the tiles sent by John Quincy to his mother as a gift to console her when John was not reelected President. Leaning against the fireplace is a bedwarmer that John and Abigail received as a wedding present. Abigail died in this room on October 28, 1818. (Courtesy of the U.S. Dept. of the Interior, National Park Service, Adams National Historic Site, Quincy, Massachusetts.)

This close-up picture of the bedwarmer shows the engraving of Abigail's name and the date of her marriage in the center. (Courtesy of the U.S. Dept. of the Interior, National Park Service, Adams National Historic Site, Quincy, Massachusetts.)

angrily in her letters of the damage and the cost and aggravation of having it repaired.

In John's and Abigail's bedroom, the tiles around their fireplace are the ones John Quincy sent them from Europe as a consolation gift when John was not reelected to the Presidency. Leaning against the fireplace is a brass bedwarmer that John and Abigail received as a wedding present. Their bed, with its summer hangings and its ornately carved footboard, fills the room. Next door is the guest room, the room where Abigail nursed her dying daughter in 1813. If you peek into the closet underneath the stairs to the servants' rooms, you can see the green and blue print wallpaper that Abigail had on the walls of her upstairs hall.

Downstairs in the kitchen area, you can see the china used by Abigail at meals. In other places are the locket John gave her before leaving for Europe, her bullet mold, and other items that Abigail used.

Abigail and John would have a long retirement life together, filled with family and friends and a great deal of writing. For Abigail it must have seemed a time of great peace finally to have her "beloved partner" at home with her, away from the demands of his career. On October 25, 1814, Abigail and John celebrated their fiftieth wedding anniversary. Even with all the years apart, their long lives allowed them more time together than many married couples of the day had. When the time came for her death on October 28, 1818, it would be with John by her side. All of Quincy would mourn her death. John would live until July 4, 1826, dying just a few hours after Thomas Jefferson on the fiftieth anniversary of the Declaration of Independence.

Chapter 18

VISIONARY

*C*harles Francis Adams, the grandson of John and Abigail, wrote a biography of his grandfather. In it he stated that in two areas of his life, John had been luckier than "most men who have lived." One was in the loyalty of his son, John Quincy Adams. The other was in his marriage to Abigail. He wrote of his grandmother and her marriage this way: "He was happily married to ... a person with a mind capable of comprehending his, with affections strong enough to respond to his sensibility, with a sympathy equal to his highest aspirations, and yet with flexibility sufficient to yield to his stronger will without impairing her own dignity."

Abigail Adams was not the typical woman of the Revolutionary War period. As a child, her education was different. She was given a freedom to learn that was most unusual for girls of the time. She was also exposed to ideas that were usually reserved for the education of boys and men.

Abigail Adams also experienced a very different role as a wife than the women of her time. Her "partnership" with John Adams was unusual and made her his equal in many parts of their relationship —

something that was absolutely unheard of in that era. John genuinely relied on Abigail for her comments and her observations on the political issues of the day. In their correspondence, they conversed as equals when they discussed issues that were not about the home. John counted on Abigail and her insights to keep him in touch with the real political feelings of the people while he was away.

John Adams's long time away from home, first for the Continental Congress and later in Europe, gave Abigail responsibilities that most women did not have. Many women of the time did share the economic responsibility for their families with their husbands. But for Abigail to be left in charge while John was out of the country for such long periods of time was very unusual for this period in our history. Usually a male relative would have been given this responsibility. At first John closely guided her decisions (in his continuously nagging letters!). Eventually, however, as he became more involved in his work in distant lands, she began to make the decisions on her own. Over time, even John recognized that she was better at managing their property than he was.

All these factors served to make Abigail Adams different from the women of her time. But they did not make her unique. What made her unique was her role as an actual participant in the political discussions of the time. She carried on a correspondence not just with John but with other political leaders. Her insights ensured that her ideas were well respected. Her participation, even as limited as it was, foreshadowed the role that women would increasingly play in the development of the new nation.

By today's standards, Abigail Adams was much too willing to downplay her own talents and her own role. She constantly spoke of her own lack of learning and importance. She did not assert herself either with John or in the political and social arena. But in her own quiet way, she showed what women were capable of doing. She was always competent but never strident.

Abigail Adams was also a visionary. She saw what women could become with education and opportunity. She continually served as an advocate for women with John. During the time of the Continental Congress, she made a strong plea for the equality of women and men. She wrote to John asking that the men "Remember the Ladies"—probably the letter for which she is still the most well-known. She argued that husbands should not be given total control over their wives, noting that "Men would be tyrants if they could." (March 31, 1776.) She also argued that by declaring men free without also declaring women free, the men were set- ting themselves up for another revolution — one in which the women would take over and demand their own freedom. Her advocacy did not change John's mind. In fact, he wrote back calling her "saucy" and said her arguments made him laugh. Abigail continued her argument in her next letter on May 7, 1776, argu- ing even more strongly this time: "I cannot say, that I think you are very generous to the ladies ... you insist upon retaining an absolute power over wives ... notwithstanding all your wise laws and maxims, we have it in our power, not only to free ourselves, but to subdue our masters, and, without violence, throw both your natural and legal authority at our feet." But John held firm to his own beliefs. John thought of Abigail as his "partner" in most things. However, he also thought of Abigail as the exception to what most women were like. Therefore he was not willing to grant women the same rights that men had.

Abigail would continue as a visionary. In her letters to friends over the years, she continued to advocate a

A photograph of one of Abigail's most famous letters to John. Written on March 31, 1776, she urges him to "Remember the Ladies, & be more generous & favourable to them than your ancestors ... remember all Men would be tyrants if they could." (Courtesy of the Massachusetts Historical Society.)

good education for women. She knew that freedom and equality would not come in her lifetime; but she also knew that having all girls acquire an education would lead to the day when women would be free of the "tyranny" of men. She would write to John on June 30, 1778, soon after he arrived in France, "But, in this country, you need not be told how much female education is neglected, nor how fashionable it has been to ridicule female learning; though I acknowledge it my happiness to be connected with a person of a more generous mind and liberal sentiments."

It would be interesting to know what Abigail would think of the freedom of women today. Abigail never advocated total freedom. Therefore she might be shocked at the changes of today. On the other hand, Abigail might be quite proud that the "revolution" she once spoke of has indeed taken place, and that women have become the equal partners in life that she always felt they should be.

SOURCES FOR RESEARCH

There are many books that have been written about Abigail Adams. However, I really wanted to tell her story through her own letters. Now that presented a problem. Abigail really was the bad speller she claimed to be. In 1848, her grandson, Charles Francis Adams, published many of Abigail's letters, correcting her spelling and grammatical errors in the process (*Letters of Mrs. Adams*). This version of the letters is much more readable, especially in a book for a younger reading audience. Because of this I chose to use this old edition of her letters, rather than the new, correct version being published by the Adams Manuscript Trust through Harvard University. In working with John Adams's letters, I have tried to remain consistent by using the version prepared by Charles Francis Adams in 1856 (*The Works of John Adams*). It is important for the reader to know, however, that there exists a newer, more original edition of these letters, which is still being worked on.

I did use the original letters quoted in *The Adams-Jefferson Letters* (ed. by Lester J. Cappon, Chapel Hill: University of North Carolina Press, 1959), which is a two volume collection of the letters between both

John and Abigail Adams and Thomas Jefferson.

By far the most interesting part of my research on Abigail Adams involved a special tour of the Adamses' homes that was given by the Curator of the Adams National Historic Site, Judith McAlister Curtis. For one memorable morning I had the opportunity to walk where Abigail had walked and to see parts of the house that are normally closed to visitors. It is a real thrill to stand looking out the window of the bedroom where Abigail died and to know you are seeing what she saw. It is inspiring to touch things she used in her own life. As Judy and I exchanged Abigail stories while walking through the houses, Abigail came alive for me in a way she never had before.

There are many excellent biographies of Abigail Adams written for the adult reader. I have enjoyed Phyllis Lee Levin's *Abigail Adams: A Biography* (New York: Ballantine Books, 1987); Paul Nagel's *Adams Women* (New York: Oxford University Press, 1987); Janet Whitney's *Abigail Adams* (Boston: Little, Brown and Company, 1947); and Charles W. Akers's *Abigail Adams: An American Woman* (Boston: Little, Brown and Company, 1980). My favorite of all, however, is still Irving Stone's biographical novel, *Those Who Love* (New York: Doubleday, 1965), which I read so many years ago.

INDEX